GREAT BOOK *of*
WOODBURNING

GREAT BOOK *of* WOODBURNING

by Lora S. Irish

Fox Chapel Publishing
1970 Broad Street • East Petersburg, PA 17520
www.FoxChapelPublishing.com

Alan Giagnocavo
Publisher

Peg Couch
Acquisition Editor

Gretchen Bacon
Editor

Troy Thorne
Book Design

Linda Eberly
Layout

ISBN-13: 978–1–56523–287–7
ISBN-10: 1–56523–287–9

Publisher's Cataloging-in-Publication Data

    Irish, Lora S.

        Great book of woodburning / by Lora S. Irish. -- East Petersburg, PA: Fox Chapel Publishing, c2006.

           p. ; cm.

           ISBN-13: 978-1-56523-287-7
           ISBN-10: 1-56523-287-9
           Includes index.

           1. Pyrography--Technique. 2. Pyrography--Patterns. 3. Woodwork--Technique. I. Title.

TT199.8 .I75 2006
745.51/4--dc22   0609

To learn more about the other great books from
Fox Chapel Publishing, or to find a retailer near you,
call toll-free 1-800-457-9112 or visit us at *www.FoxChapelPublishing.com*.

Note to Authors: We are always looking for talented
authors to write new books in our area of woodworking, design,
and related crafts. Please send a brief letter describing your idea to
Peg Couch, Acquisition Editor, 1970 Broad Street, East Petersburg, PA 17520.

Printed in China
10 9 8 7 6 5 4 3 2 1

Dedication

This work is dedicated to Michael, my beloved husband and best friend, who has encouraged and emotionally supported me in so many loving ways through my life's journey as a fine artist.

Acknowledgments

I would like to extend my deepest appreciation to the team at Fox Chapel Publishing—especially to Alan, Peg, Gretchen, Troy, and Linda. It is a true delight to work with such a professional group dedicated to creating the best books and instruction manuals possible.

Contents

About the Author

Lora S. Irish is a nationally known artist and author, whose books include *Landscapes in Relief*, *Wildlife Carving in Relief*, *North American Wildlife Patterns for the Scroll Saw*, *World Wildlife Patterns for the Scroll Saw*, *Great Book of Dragon Patterns*, *Great Book of Fairy Patterns*, *Great Book of Floral Patterns*, and *Wood Spirits and Green Men*. She is also a frequent contributor to *Woodcarving Illustrated* and *Scroll Saw Woodworking & Crafts*. Twelve of the author's purebred dog breed oil canvas paintings have been published as limited editions.

Working from their home studio, Lora and her husband and webmaster, Michael, are the owners of two websites: Fine Art Dog Prints, *www.muttart.com,* and Classic Carving Patterns, *www.carvingpatterns.com*. Their online art gallery, Fine Art Dog Prints, features the works of over 60 canine artists. Classic Carving Patterns is their Internet woodcarving studio focusing on online tutorials, projects, and patterns created exclusively by the author for the crafter and artisan.

Introduction

Whether you've never tried pyrography before or you've simply used it to sign or enhance projects created in other media, this book will show you how to create beautiful pieces with only a pyrographic tool. Today's pyrographic equipment can be both inexpensive and readily available, so getting started is easy to do.

Although it is often referred to as woodburning, the art of pyrography can be worked on just about any natural surface, which gives you a wide variety of possibilities on which to explore this craft. Wooden box tops, gourd bluebird houses, watercolor paper that's suitable for framing, and even leather belts are used as working surfaces for burned designs. For this book, I worked the finished samples on several different species of wood, such as birch plywood and basswood. However, the techniques and instruction do apply to other materials, such as leather, paper, and gourds.

As you work through the lessons, ideas, and patterns in this book, you will learn how to start with a drawing or a photograph and translate it to a fully finished, finely detailed woodburned project. Working step-by-step, we will explore what materials and tools you will need for your woodburning kit, which woods might best suit your project, how to prepare the wood surface and transfer your patterns, how to judge the depth of color or tonal value for each area of your design, and of course, how to create and control the woodburned tonal values through the use of textures and layers. Once your woodburning is complete, we will focus on how to add color to the burning as well as what top finishes you may wish to use.

You will also notice, as you browse through the pages, that the step-by-step projects and the patterns are broken into beginner, intermediate, and advanced sections. This breakdown of patterns and projects is designed to get you started in woodburning and to provide you with ideas and patterns to match your skill level as you continue to grow in your art. The projects are presented so that you can learn not only how to woodburn a design or pattern but also why a particular technique, tonal value, or texture was used. With the basic instructions in this book and a little practice, you will soon be able to woodburn any drawing, pattern, or photograph with confidence and expertise.

What is Pyrography?

Pyrography: The art of burning a design or pattern into a natural surface, such as wood, gourds, leather, or cotton rag watercolor paper using heated one-temperature or variable-temperature woodburning tools or a fine flame.

Pyrographic Process: The action of creating a detailed drawing onto a natural surface by using a woodburning tool to control the depth and thickness of the burned line and to develop tonal depths of shading. Pyrographic designs and patterns include landscapes, house portraits, dragons, comical firemen, wall clocks, wild roses, cowboy boots, old cars, flying mallard ducks, Western horses, and many other subjects.

Pyrographer: The person who gets to have all of the fun, excitement, and enjoyment of creating those burned drawings on clocks, box lids, jewelry, gourd birdhouses, tabletops, bookshelves, door hangers, Christmas ornaments, leather key holders, belts, cowboy chaps, greeting cards, framed art, and much more!

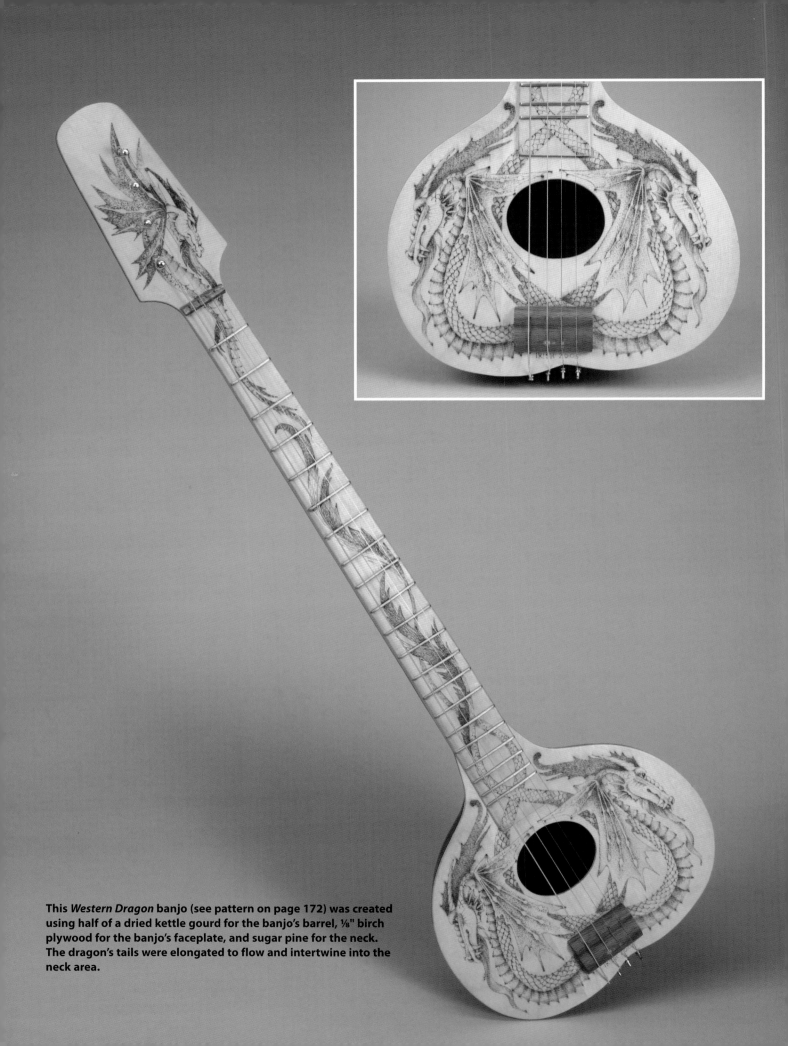

This *Western Dragon* banjo (see pattern on page 172) was created using half of a dried kettle gourd for the banjo's barrel, ⅛" birch plywood for the banjo's faceplate, and sugar pine for the neck. The dragon's tails were elongated to flow and intertwine into the neck area.

Gallery

Once you learn how easy it is to create a stunning and dramatic woodburned design, you will discover a wide variety of project surfaces that are perfect for your next burning. In this gallery section, I will share a few of my ideas, including a gourd banjo, thumb drums, a basswood boat oar, and even an office desk set.

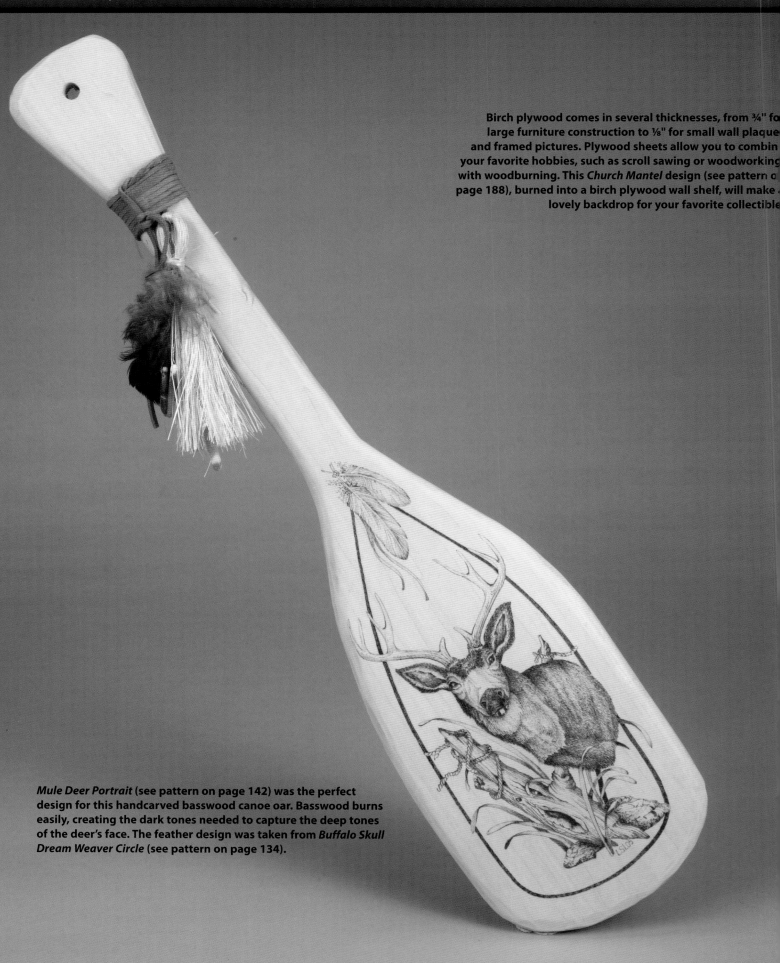

Birch plywood comes in several thicknesses, from ¾" fo
large furniture construction to ⅛" for small wall plaque
and framed pictures. Plywood sheets allow you to combin
your favorite hobbies, such as scroll sawing or woodworking
with woodburning. This *Church Mantel* design (see pattern o
page 188), burned into a birch plywood wall shelf, will make a
lovely backdrop for your favorite collectible

Mule Deer Portrait (see pattern on page 142) was the perfect
design for this handcarved basswood canoe oar. Basswood burns
easily, creating the dark tones needed to capture the deep tones
of the deer's face. The feather design was taken from *Buffalo Skull
Dream Weaver Circle* (see pattern on page 134).

Woodburning is perfect for outdoor decorations, such as house signs (see *White-Tailed Deer Lodge* pattern on page 144), deck chairs, and wooden planters. Once burned, the brown colors of the design are permanent and weatherproof.

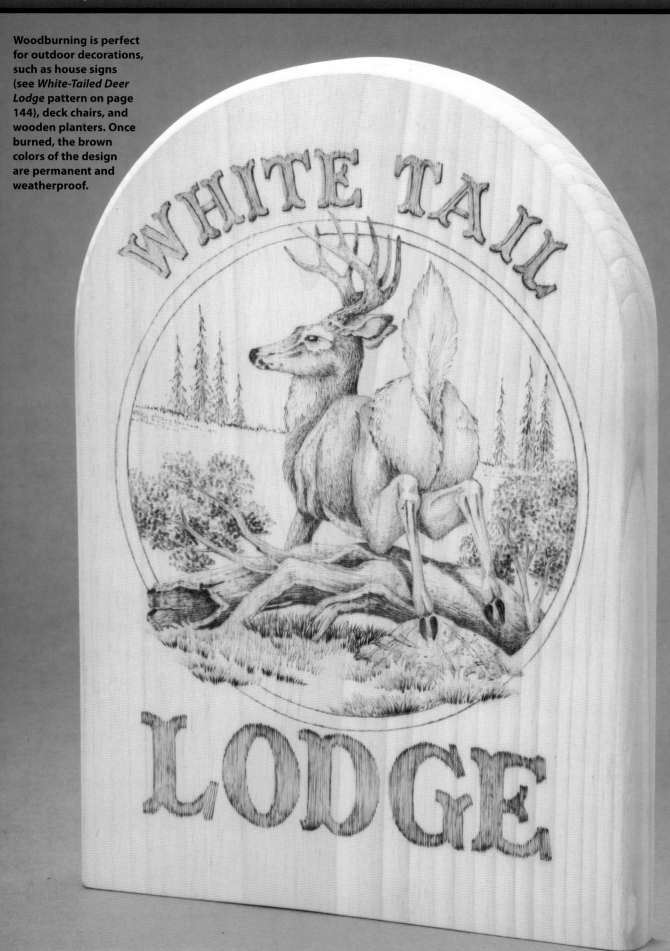

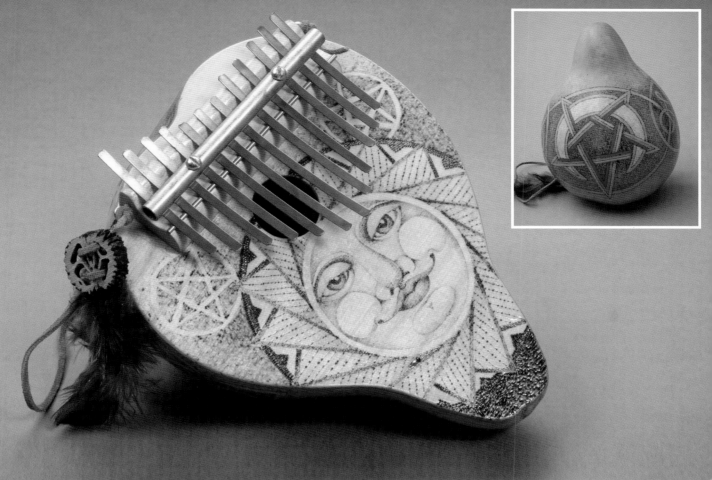

A large dried kettle gourd, ⅛" birch plywood, and a key set were used to create the thumb drum of *Summer Morning Sun Face/Pentagram Star* (top and inset) and the thumb drum of *American Eagle* (bottom right and left). These would make wonderful gifts for your burgeoning musician (see patterns on pages 115, 116, and 146).

The *Berry Green Man* has been worked on a desk envelope holder (see pattern on page 148). His dark eyes are accented by the dark shadows on the leaf and berry areas.

The *Oak Man* was used on the stationary/file holder box as the second piece of this desk set (see pattern on page 150). The back of the box is tall enough to include a small secondary accent of leaves.

Part 1

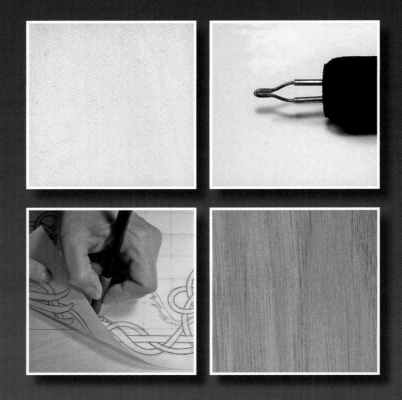

Woodburning Basics

Woodburning as an art form has many benefits. In addition to being a wonderful way for an artist to express himself or herself, the tools and materials are rather minimal when compared to other art forms like woodcarving and woodturning. In this part of the book, we'll take a look at the tools and equipment you'll need to get started woodburning and address how to keep them in top running order.

Woodburning Tools and Equipment

Pyrography as a craft has one distinct advantage over any other art form or hobby I know: It is very inexpensive to get started. Once you have purchased your choice of woodburning tool, your hobby costs will be limited to new project surfaces on which to work your burning and new pattern or technique books to add to your pyrography library. The basic woodburning tool will last through many years of hard use.

Woodburners/pyrographic machines

There are two styles of woodburning tools. The most basic style is a one-temperature tool that heats to a pre-set temperature and uses solid brass interchangeable burning tips. The second style is the variable-temperature tool. This type of burner includes an adjustable thermostat unit and plug-in woodburning pens that can have either fixed pen tips or interchangeable tips. We will explore the advantages of both types of burners.

One-Temperature Tool with Interchangeable Solid Brass Tips

This style of woodburning tool is excellent for beginning woodburners because it is readily available at your local arts and craft store and is extremely inexpensive. My first woodburning tool was a one-temperature tool with interchangeable tips, and I have used it for over twenty years (see **Figure 1.1**). Several years ago, I added a second one-temperature tool so that I could have two tools at hand for any project to cut down on my need to change tips.

The one-temperature tool has a burning pen that contains the heating element. At the top of the pen is a screw receptacle where the interchangeable tips are secured. The interchangeable tips are made from brass, threaded at their base, and attached to the front end of the woodburning tool. When this tool is plugged into a wall outlet, it heats to a single temperature: high.

Most one-temperature tools are sold with several different tip styles. The most common brass tip is called a universal tip. It can be used for both

Figure 1.1. This one-temperature tool heats to one setting: high. It comes with several interchangeable tips.

Heating element area

Grip

Heat shield

Tip receptacle

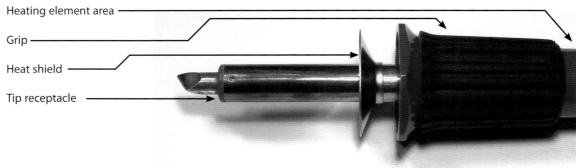

Figure 1.2. Several different solid brass tips are included with a basic one-temperature woodburning tool. This basic set provides enough profiles to create outstanding, well-shaded, and detailed burnings with a wide variety of tonal values.

Interchangeable brass tips

Universal tip

Calligraphy tip

Flow tip

Cone tip

Large shading tip

fine-line work as well as shading work. The other common tips that are available for this style of woodburner are the calligraphy tip, which is used for lettering; the flow tip, which is used for large area fills; the cone tip, which creates fine detailing; and the large shading tip, which burns large areas and shadows (see **Figure 1.2**).

This style of tool does have several disadvantages. Most importantly, the one-temperature tool heats to only one high temperature, which means that various color tones need to be created through several different burning techniques as opposed to changing heat settings (see **Figure 1.3**). The tool can also become very hot while you work, forcing you to take short breaks during long burning sessions.

The greatest advantage to the one-temperature woodburning tool is its low cost. It is extremely inexpensive, so for just a few dollars spent at your local hobby or craft store, you can get started in this art form. For many beginning woodburners, this advantage alone is often enough to overcome the disadvantages mentioned above.

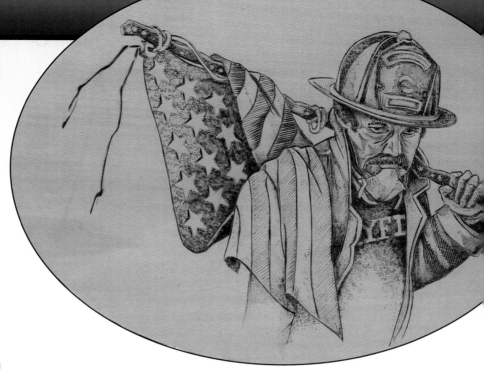

Variable-Temperature Tool with Interchangeable and Fixed Wire Tips

As my love of woodburning grew, I soon decided that I wanted to add a variable-temperature, or thermostat, tool to my kit (see **Figure 1.4**). The woodburning system I chose included a variable-temperature burner, three pens (two permanently fixed wire-tip pens and one interchangeable tip pen), and an assortment of twenty interchangeable wire tips. For the beginning woodburner, the different heat settings make it quick and easy to change color tones within a project.

Figure 1.3. This design, *New York's Finest*, was burned using a one-temperature woodburner. Because this style of tool has only one high setting, the shading was controlled by how slowly or quickly the line was burned and by how many lines fill one area.

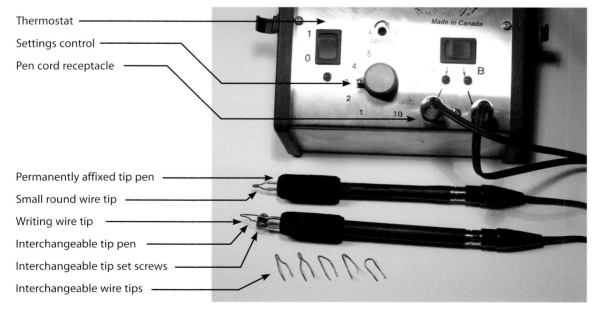

Thermostat
Settings control
Pen cord receptacle

Permanently affixed tip pen
Small round wire tip
Writing wire tip
Interchangeable tip pen
Interchangeable tip set screws
Interchangeable wire tips

Figure 1.4. Variable-temperature woodburners include a base thermostat that can be adjusted for a wide range of temperatures, from very cool to extremely hot. The tools are available with either fixed or interchangeable tips.

Figure 1.5. With just a few assorted tip styles the variable-temperature tool will create a wide variety of tonal values, line widths, and textures.

Variable-temperature burning tools are more expensive than the one-temperature tools. Often, the cost of a basic set-up, which includes the thermostat unit and several fixed-tip pens, begins around $200. These types of woodburning tools may need to be purchased through a specialty store or directly through the manufacturer.

The thermostat unit for a variable-temperature woodburner can be set for any temperature range from very cool, at setting number 1, to extremely hot, at setting number 10. This type of wood-burner will reach temperatures that are suitable for many other hobbies besides woodburning, such as stencil cutting and metal etching. The burning pens are plugged directly into the thermostat and have plenty of electrical cord for easy use at your worktable.

Figure 1.6. This is an interchangeable tip pen for the variable-temperature tool. The wire tips are secured to the pen using set screws. Interchangeable tip pens do not conduct the heat quite as evenly as fixed pens do, however they are an excellent choice for specialty tips that you may only use on occasion.

Figure 1.7. *American Eagle* was worked using a wire loop tip on a variable-temperature woodburner. Variable-temperature tools change temperature quickly, making it easy to get a smooth work flow.

Variable-temperature woodburning pens are available with either interchangeable wire tips or permanently affixed wire tips. A basic selection of interchangeable tips includes a writing tip, a small or fine writing tip, a small round tip, a flat shader, and a large wire loop tip (see **Figure 1.5**). These tips will work well for 90 percent of your burning projects. (The majority of the burning projects in this book were done using only the writing tip and the small round tip.) Because I use a large writing tip most often, I chose to purchase a fixed-tip pen with this tip.

Special interchangeable tips are available with profiles for very specific purposes (see **Figure 1.6**). Fish scale wire tips can be obtained in many different sizes and shapes depending on the fish pattern you are burning. Feather tips, circles, and squares are also easy to find.

Most tips for this type of woodburning pen, whether permanently affixed or interchangeable, are created with wire that is bent into the different tip profiles. The tool tip changes temperatures quickly with little waiting time between heat adjustments. This means you can move from a low heat setting to a higher setting within a few seconds, keeping a smooth work flow during a burning session (see **Figure 1.7**).

Other tools

In addition to your woodburning tool, there are several other items you will want to gather into your woodburning kit before you start your first project (see **Figure 1.8**).

Foam-core emery boards, *200- to 250-grit sandpaper*, and *silicon carbide cloths* all serve several purposes in woodburning kits. They are used to keep your tool tips of the one-temperature tools clean from carbon build-up, which we will discuss in Keeping Your Tool Tips Clean on page 17. Finer grade sandpapers or emery cloths give a smoother polish to your tip, which ensures more even, consistent heating for your burned lines. A *leather strop and aluminum oxide honing compound* will also work to keep your tool tips clean. Regardless of what type of tool you choose, you will also be using sandpaper to prepare the wood surface for the pattern tracing and to sand lightly after the burning is completed.

A *white artist's eraser* is excellent for removing the pattern tracing lines and guidelines that you will use during the burning work. Avoid using erasers that are colored, such as the large, pink, office-supply style. These erasers can leave their color behind on the wood. The colored streaks are permanent and require sanding to remove them.

A variety of *graphite pencils*, from a #H to #2B hard pencil through a #4B to #6B soft pencil, should be added to the kit. The harder grades of pencil, #H to #2B, are used for tracing the pattern lines. Soft pencils, #4B to #6B, can be used to coat the back of your pattern to create graphite tracings. Throw a roll of *masking tape* and *transparent tape* into the kit to secure the paper patterns to your board.

Tool tips need to be changed during the burning work. For variable-temperature tools, a *small*

What you'll need

- Several grades of foam-core emery boards
- 200- to 250-grit sandpaper and/or silicon carbide cloths (emery cloth)
- Leather strop and aluminum oxide honing compound
- White artist's eraser
- Graphite pencils, #H to #2B hard pencil through #4B to #6B soft pencil
- Masking tape and/or transparent tape
- Small screwdriver (for variable-temperature tools)
- Needle-nose pliers (for one-temperature tools)
- Small round woodcarving gouge
- Lint-free cloths or a large drafter's dusting brush
- Metal ruler or straightedge
- T-square and/or 90-degree drafter's triangle
- Vellum tracing paper or onionskin tracing paper
- Artist-quality colored pencils
- Artist-quality watercolor paints and brushes
- Artist-quality oil paints and brushes
- Polyurethane spray sealer, tung oil, or Danish oil finish
- Paste wax

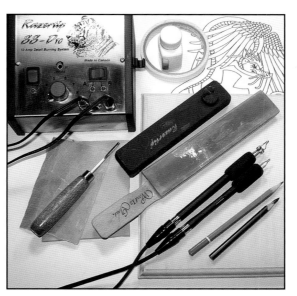

Figure 1.8.
After you've chosen your woodburner, you'll need a few other supplies, including pencils, an eraser, and sandpaper.

screwdriver will do the job. One-temperature tools will require a pair of *needle-nose pliers*.

A *small round woodcarving gouge* is great to have handy. We all make mistakes. Sometime during a woodburning you will invariably burn the wrong area or burn an area too dark. Using a small round woodcarving gouge, you can gently carve away the incorrect burning, lightly sand to remove any marks left by the gouge, and then re-burn that area correctly.

To remove the dust left behind during the sanding steps and to remove the waste created from using the white artist's eraser, you will need either *lint-free cloths or a large drafter's dusting brush*.

For guidelines and pattern placement, you will need a *metal ruler or a straightedge* plus a *T-square and/or a 90-degree drafter's triangle*. My kit includes all of these. Choose a metal ruler, not plastic, so you can use it to guide the woodburning tool as you work. (**Note:** Plastic rulers and the plastic edges of a T-square can melt if used as a tool guide.) An artist's straightedge has an advantage over the common ruler because it does not have the measurement marks along the edge. This allows the woodburning tip to glide smoothly along that edge without catching or wobbling because of the measurement indents. Many straightedges come with a thin layer of corkboard on the bottom, which prevents the straightedge from sliding or moving when in use. If you do use a measuring instrument to help you burn straight lines, remember that they will decrease the temperature of your tool tip, so you may need to repeat the burned line several times. Drafter's triangles are especially handy for check-ing traced lines that meet at square angles, such as a barn wall and roof joint area. Because they are made from transparent plastic, you can see

your pattern lines through the drafter's triangle. For longer square angles and for proper place-ment of the pattern on a wood board, use the T-square. The T of the T-square can be placed along the side or edge of the wood board, and the pattern lines can be adjusted using the ruler leg of the T-square, ensuring that your pattern is properly squared to the board.

To transfer your pattern onto the wood surface, you will want either *vellum tracing paper or onionskin tracing paper*. I prefer vellum paper because it has the same transparent qualities found in onionskin paper; however, vellum is readily available in large sheet sizes. Transferring a pattern with onionskin paper can require several sheets taped together.

Artist-quality colored pencils are often used to add colored details to a finished work. There are two grades of colored pencils available on the market today: student grade and artist grade. Student-grade pencils have a high content of chalk and wax as their base. This can cause a cloudy or milky effect that will block out all of your woodburning work. Instead, invest in a set of artist-quality colored pencils. These have a much smaller chalk and wax content and are more transparent. Many artist colored pencils are also lightfast. Because colored pencils can be mixed by laying one layer of color over another to create new hues, a set of 12 or 24 pencils will do excellently. Artist colored pencils are available in three styles: dry (chalk) colored pencils, oil colored pencils, and watercolor pencils. Which style of colored pencils you choose depends upon your wood preference and coloring style. Dry colored pencils are used to fill in the coloring in each area and have a somewhat transparent look. Oil colored pencils are similar to oil pastels and build up in the woodburned texture quickly. They are applied dry, but, because of the oil content, they can be blended with the use of a blending tortillon or a small oxen-hair brush. Watercolor pencils are also applied dry. Once the color coverage has been achieved, you can use a soft sable brush and water to moisten the colors for blending and shading, exactly as you would when using watercolor paints.

Artist-quality watercolors and *oil paints* are also used as coloring agents. Watercolors, which are available in either tube or cake form, are most often used on woods such as basswood and pine, where they can soak into the fibers of the wood. They are extremely transparent, allowing all of your woodburning tonal values to show through the coloring, and are easily blended to create new colors and shading tones. *Soft sable brushes* are used to apply watercolors, and a glass tile or plate makes a good palette. Oil paints are used for harder woods, such as birch, maple, or walnut, and can easily be blended for new hues. Mixed with turpentine and linseed oil, oil paints can be made into very transparent glazes that work wonderfully to add coloring. When glaze painting with oil paints, use soft sable brushes. Both of these types of artist colors are available in sets of 6 to 12 basic colors.

Polyurethane spray sealer, tung oil or Danish oil, and *paste wax* are great for sealing woodburnings. Polyurethane spray sealer works well for woodburn-ings with color because the spray does not disturb the color. Tung oil and Danish oil provide a very hard finish and help to bring out the natural beauty of uncolored woodburnings. Paste wax creates a soft-looking sheen over uncolored woodburnings.

Keeping your tool tips clean

As you work with a woodburning tool, whether it is a one-temperature tool or a variable temperature tool, carbon deposits will begin to build up on the tool tip. The hotter the temperature, the quicker the deposits will develop. This black build-up can

be transferred to your work, causing dark gray or black streaks that cannot be removed. Heavy carbon deposits can also affect the temperature of the tool tip, causing the tip to cool below its normal heat setting. Unevenly burned lines that vary sharply in color or width are most often caused by a dirty tip. You will want to check your tool tip often and clean it whenever this build-up becomes noticeable. When the tool tip starts to take on a chocolate-brown tone, unplug the tool. Allow the tool to cool for about 10 minutes. Then, use one of the following three methods for cleaning your tool tip. Do not attempt to clean hot tips, whether solid brass or wire, because this can damage the metal and the cleaning surface.

The first way to clean your tool tip is to use fine-grit sandpaper to polish the brass tip of a one-temperature pen back to a bright, shiny finish (see **Figure 1.9**). Use either a small sheet of 220- to 250-grit sandpaper or a foam-core emery board for this task. Once the carbon has been removed, you can add an extra fine polish to the face of the brass tip using silicon carbide cloth (emery cloth), which is available in very fine grits of 400 and higher. This method will not work for wire tips because they are too delicate to withstand sandpaper cleaning.

Using a honing strop and aluminum oxide honing compound is the second way to clean tool tips, and it works for both one-temperature and variable-temperature tips (see **Figure 1.10**). A small amount of the compound is placed on the strop; then, the tool tip is pulled across the strop's surface to clear the tip of carbon. This is my favorite cleaning method because it does the least amount of damage to any tool tips while restoring them to the bright finish that creates clean burned strokes.

The third method can be used with the variable-temperature tool. Some manufacturers create a scraping tool that will be packaged with your variable-temperature woodburner. This scraping tool has a sharp metal edge over which the wire tip can be dragged to clean off the carbon (see **Figure 1.11**).

Figure 1.9. Very fine grade sandpaper or emery cloth can be used to keep your one-temperature tool's solid brass tips bright and clean. The paper used here is 400-grit emery cloth.

Figure 1.10. This variable-temperature tool tip is being cleaned on a honing board using aluminum oxide compound. The leather honing strop has been prepared with red oxide compound and is ready to clean either variable-temperature wire tips or the solid brass tips of the one-temperature tool.

Figure 1.11. Some variable-temperature tool units include a wire tip tool scraper for cleaning.

Selecting Wood for Woodburning

A large variety of wood species make wonderful backgrounds for woodburning. The most common are basswood, white birch, and white pine. These three woods can easily be purchased from craft and hobby supply stores in precut, prerouted shapes or as unfinished furniture. Butternut, walnut, and mahogany are also favorites of woodburners; however, they are not commonly found in precut shapes. These woods can be obtained through woodworking supply stores as lumber stock.

Each species of wood has its own properties when burned, depending on the softness or hardness of the wood, the spacing of the grain, and the saw cut direction of each particular piece. Softer woods, such as basswood and white pine, burn more easily than harder wood species, like white birch. For example, a woodburning on basswood done at the same temperature setting and stroke pressure will be much

deeper in color tone than one done on white birch. The width of the burned line will also be thicker on softer woods, compared to the tight lines burned into harder woods.

Features to consider

A number of features come into play when you are choosing wood for a woodburning project. Following are several elements that you'll want to consider before purchasing a piece of wood.

Hard Wood or Soft Wood?

Each type of wood—soft or hard—has unique advantages for the finished project. If you want a dark-toned, dramatic woodburning, choose a soft wood. Basswood can be burned to a rich black coloring, and white pine reaches a very dark chocolate tone. If, instead, you wish to create a woodburning with a wide range of color tones, use a harder wood as your burning surface. A hard wood such as white birch allows for extremely pale coloring, making it ideal for more complex shading schemes (see **Figure 1.12**).

Fine Grain or Coarse Grain?

The width and darkness of the grain of your wood piece also affect the finish of your woodburning. Finely grained woods, such as basswood and white birch, show very little color change in a burned line (see **Figure 1.13**). Because their grain is so closely packed and there is little color change between the grain lines, these two woods provide a clean, even surface for your work. White pine, however, is different. The grain lines in this wood are very distinct, both in width and in coloring. As you burn across the grain of white pine, you will see your burned line change in

Figure 1.12. Working the same pattern (*Dragonette*) on two different species of wood shows how the wood affects the burning. The upper burning was done on white birch plywood, a hard wood. The lower burning was done on basswood, a soft wood. Notice how the hard wood shows the pale tones, while the soft wood creates darker, thicker lines.

color tone as well as in width. This can easily be adjusted by lightly re-burning the pale areas of the line and matching them to the darker tones of the grain areas.

Plain Grain or End Grain?

Wood boards can be cut from the tree log in several ways. Plain-grain wood is cut from the old growth rings and runs vertical to the growth of the tree rings. End-grain wood is cut horizontal to the tree and so includes the central heart section outward to the bark (see **Figure 1.14**). Growth rings close to the heart of the tree are darker in appearance and are usually wider than the outer growth rings. Heartwood contains a higher sap content than outer-growth-ring wood. Plain-grain wood, therefore, has a finer and lighter-colored grain pattern, thus creating less distortion in your woodburning.

High Sap Contents or Low Sap Contents?

The amount of sap that any particular wood contains can affect the evenness of your woodburned lines. Heavy-sap-content grain burns darker than light-sap-content areas. Since some woods contain grain areas of both low and high sap content, the burned sections of a pattern can vary dramatically. High sap content will also cause excessive carbon build-up on your tip. Clean your tool more often if you are working with high-sap-content wood. Pine is especially noted as a high-sap-content wood, and you can easily see the darker areas of grain mixed with the low-content, pale grain areas.

Light Wood or Dark Wood?

The natural coloring of the wood species also determines the final effect of your burning project. White woods, such as basswood and birch, will allow a greater color range in tonal value than darker woods, like butternut or mahogany.

Untreated or Pretreated?

I suggest that you avoid burning any wood that has been pretreated with preservatives, such as pressure-treated lumber. These preservatives are toxic and can be released into the air as you work. Painted and stained wood also can release toxic fumes when burned since many paints include lead, cadmium, and other heavy metals in their composition. Aged pieces of wood can carry molds and fungi deep within their fibers. As a general rule, it is best to work with clean, fresh, untreated wood as your woodburning background.

Figure 1.14. *Western Horse* was worked on an end-grain basswood plaque. Looking from the center of the plaque outward to the edge, you can see the tree heart in the cheek area of the horse, the old growth rings of white wood, the new growth ring of beige-colored wood, and the outer ring of bark.

Figure 1.13. *Goldfish* has been burned on a piece of heartwood birch plywood. This particular surface contains several swirls in the grain pattern that imply ripples or currents of water. Although the grain color changes dramatically, the quality of burning stays the same across the surface of this wood.

Wood species

There are many woods that can be woodburned and are readily available to the hobby wood-burner. We'll take a look at basswood, birch, pine, and butternut, just a few of the choices. Remember to choose wood based on the aspects and their impact on your project. The color of the wood and its grain pattern can be used to enhance the burned image. For finely detailed and heavily value-toned burnings, use a wood with a pale, even coloring and with little grain pattern, such as birch or basswood. However, for a more dramatic effect, you may wish to work on a wood with a strong grain line pattern or one that has a particular color, such as heartwood birch, butternut, or pine. When you are planning a woodburning project, consider the wood's hardness or softness, its color, and its grain pattern as part of the design work.

Basswood

Basswood, although listed as a hardwood species, is an extremely soft wood that is used in both woodcarving and woodburning (see **Figure 1.15**). It is readily available through craft and hobby supply stores and is often precut as plaques, boxes, and routed shapes. This species is a favorite of woodburners because its grain lines are minimal. Woodburnings on basswood do tend toward the darker tones due to the softness of the wood fibers. Basswood accepts colored pencil very well but does not do well with oil paints or stains.

Basswood, End Grain

Basswood also is readily available as end-grain plaques (see **Figure 1.16**). These plaques are sliced from the log so that the saw cut runs across the tree rings instead of with the grain. Many end-grain plaques include the outer circle

Figure 1.15. Basswood is a soft wood. Woodburnings on this wood tend to be darker due to the softness of the wood. The very pale cream color of basswood and its lack of distinct grain lines make it a perfect background for very detailed, heavily shaded designs.

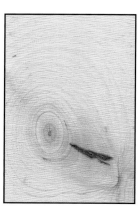

Figure 1.16. When you cut a log in slices, you get what's commonly called end grain, in which the circular pattern of the grain is visible. End grain plaques do not burn quite as evenly as plain grain wood, but the circular growth ring grain can add an interesting touch to any pattern.

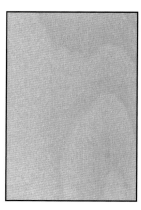

Figure 1.17. White birch plywood is a hard wood that gives a wide range of shading. The grain lines are noticeable but do not cause distortion in your woodburned strokes.

Figure 1.18. Heartwood comes from the center of the tree (this is birch) and is usually darker in color than other cuts. The tight bands create interesting backgrounds for woodburning.

Figure 1.19. White pine has a distinct grain with deep lines running through the wood, which may affect the consistency of your woodburned lines.

of bark, giving the plaque a natural frame (see Figure 1.14 on page 19). End-grain plaques often have imperfections in the wood and in the heartwood, which will show through your final burning. End-grain wood of any species does not color as well as plain grain, either with colored pencils or with paints.

Birch

White birch plywood works wonderfully for woodburning projects (see **Figure 1.17**). It is a harder wood than basswood, creating a wider range of possible burned color tones. The grain lines in birch are more noticeable than in basswood yet are pale enough to cause very little distortion to the final burning. Plywood created from birch is available in a wide variety of thicknesses, from ¹⁄₁₆" veneer to the ⅝"-thick plywood used in furniture construction. Colored pencils or oil paints are usually used on birch as a coloring agent. This wood tends to be too hard to accept watercolor work.

Birch, Heartwood Grain

This sample of birch plywood was cut from an area near the heart of the tree (see **Figure 1.18**). Heartwood in any wood species is darker in coloring and has tighter grain lines than saw cuts made along the outer growth areas of the tree. These tighter, darker bands of grain can create interesting backgrounds for your woodburnings.

White Pine and Sugar Pine

Like basswood, white pine is a common wood used in craft projects and precut shapes (see **Figure 1.19**). Unfinished wood furniture is often manufactured in clear white pine, providing the woodburner with larger project surfaces. White pine has a distinct grain with deep lines running throughout the wood. As white pine ages, it will transform into a deep gold coloring or patina, which can affect the coloring of your woodburning. Sugar pine is not as common as white pine. This species has the same woodworking properties of white pine but has a less distinct and tighter grain. White pine and sugar pine will accept colored pencils, watercolors, and oil paints as coloring agents for your woodburning. However, over time, the dark wood grain lines will reappear through the color work.

White Pine, Sapwood

Like the sample of birch heartwood, this white pine sapwood sample was cut close to the center of the tree's heart (see **Figure 1.20**). This gives the wood wide bands of grain. White pine sapwood also tends to have more imperfections than clear white pine for which you will need to adjust your burning as you work.

Butternut

Butternut is most commonly used in woodcarving but does make a beautiful background for your woodburning projects (see **Figure 1.21**). This wood can be found in precut shapes through woodcarving supply stores. Butternut has a distinctive grain, like white pine, with deep brown lines running through the medium beige color of the wood. When varnished or polyurethaned, butternut takes on a silvery-gray glow.

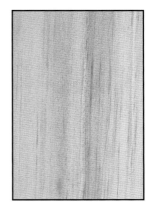

Figure 1.20. This white pine sapwood sample was cut close to the center of the tree heart, giving it wider bands of grain and imperfections that may need to be worked into your woodburning pattern or avoided.

Figure 1.21. Butternut has a distinctive grain. Deep brown lines run through medium beige wood giving your finished work an interesting appearance.

Preparing the Surface

To get the best woodburned illustration possible, you will need to do a few things before you can actually start woodburning. These tasks include preparing the surface for woodburning and applying a pattern.

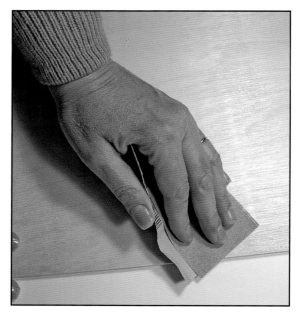

Figure 1.22. A light sanding using 250-grit sandpaper creates a smooth surface for burning. Dust the board well before proceeding.

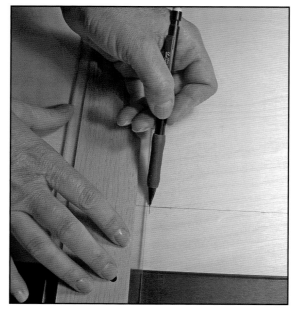

Figure 1.23. A T-square, a metal ruler, or a drafter's triangle can be used to create pattern placement guidelines on your wood surface.

Preparing a wood surface for burning

To show you how to prepare a wood surface for burning, I am working on birch plywood, preparing to burn *Dragonette Chessboard*. Although the plywood is very smooth, I prefer to start any work with a light sanding using 250-grit sandpaper (see **Figure 1.22**). Just a light sanding is usually enough. When this step is complete, wipe the board clean of dust with a lint-free cloth or large drafter's dusting brush.

Many designs that you burn will require careful placement on your wood project. A ruler, a 90-degree drafter's triangle, and a T-square are excellent tools to have at hand. For the chessboard, I have marked a two-inch border along each side of the plywood (see **Figure 1.23**). This borderline will be where the outside dimension lines of the actual chessboard squares will lie.

As you begin to make pencil marks on your project, remember that any pencil lines, tracing lines, or carbon paper lines that are on your wood during the burning process can become permanently affixed if the tool tip crosses those lines. The heat of the tool tip burns the pencil graphite or carbon paper into the wood fibers, so it is best to avoid any excess pencil graphite during the tracing process. Be sure to keep the pencil lines light in color by using gentle pressure. Light-colored graphite can be burned over without affecting the finished look of the work. Heavy or dark pencil lines should be erased or lightened with an eraser just before burning.

Tracing the pattern

For this large design, I first make a tracing of the pattern from the book on transparent vellum. Remember to trace only those lines that you need for guidance during burning so that you don't have excess graphite on your board. If, for example, you are tracing a clump of grass, you do not need to transfer a line for every grass blade. You will probably only need to transfer the outer lines of the clump.

Next, I turn the vellum upside down and, on the back, retrace the design using a very soft #2 pencil (see **Figure 1.24**). This retraced pattern will become the pencil lines that I will transfer to the plywood board. (Using the back of the vellum means that my design will not become reversed when I transfer it to the wood.) When I have completed this step, my vellum paper will have a pencil copy of the pattern on both the front and the back sides.

The type of paper, whether vellum, onionskin, or 20- to 24-pound bond paper (printer paper), will determine how easy the second tracing on the back of the pattern will be. Vellum and onionskin tracing papers are very translucent. When you turn your tracing paper over, you will easily see the first tracing through the back of the paper. Bond paper, common typing paper, or computer printer paper are not as transparent as vellum. For these heavier papers, you can use a light box. The pattern is laid face down (first tracing side down) onto the light box glass. The light then shines through the paper, making the first tracing visible. Large patterns worked on heavier paper can be taped to the glass of a window or patio door on a sunny day. Place the first tracing side of the pattern to the glass. The sunshine will now come through the pattern paper revealing the pattern lines.

Resizing the pattern

If you want your finished burning to be the same size as the patterns in this book, you can use vellum or onionskin paper laid directly over the pattern for your tracing steps. To create patterns that are larger or smaller than the ones shown here, you may wish to have a copy made with a copier. Most copier machines allow you to adjust the size of the copy that is being made. Many libraries, printing shops, and office supply stores have copying services. Computer scanners can also be used for quick, easy copies of these patterns. Once you have scanned the pattern into the computer, you can print a copy with your computer's printer. With a graphics program, you can change the size of the scanned image to create larger and smaller versions of these designs.

Figure 1.24. Turn your tracing vellum to the back and use a soft pencil to trace over the pattern lines.

Transferring the pattern to the wood

Following the marked two-inch border guidelines that you placed using the T-square, position the vellum tracing paper on the plywood, matching the edge line of the pattern to the two-inch borderline. Place masking tape along the sides of the tracing paper to adhere it to the plywood. Use your thumbnail to rub over the pattern lines (see **Figure 1.25**). The force of your thumbnail will make the pencil tracing on the back of the vellum tracing paper rub off onto the plywood, creating your pencil lines for burning.

Note: For this step, you can also use the point of your pencil or an ink pen to transfer the lines to the wood. Here the pencil or pen will force the graphite onto the wood. Work carefully if you do use a pencil or an ink pen since these can leave a fine-line impression in softer woods such as basswood.

Because only the pattern lines were traced on the back of the tracing paper, the final pattern on your wood will be clean of smudges or streaks of excess graphite. To check how well your pattern has transferred, free one or two sides of the masking tape (see **Figure 1.26**). Leaving the remaining sides taped keeps the pattern securely in place as you check your results. If some lines are pale, simply re-rub that area. Remove any graphite smudges or streaks with a white artist's eraser before woodburning.

For the second tracing sample, I rubbed the entire back surface of my pattern paper with a soft #4B to #6B pencil (see **Figure 1.27**). When the back has an even, dark layer of graphite, I tape the pattern to the wood surface using masking tape. Then, I trace the lines with a pencil or an ink pen. The pressure from the pencil or pen transfers the graphite to the wood. Again, as with the first style of transferring a pattern, I loosen one or two edges of masking tape to check for any areas that I might have missed or that need

to be retraced. This method may leave smudges of graphite on your board where your hand rubbed against the pattern paper. These smudged areas can easily be cleaned with a white eraser.

Whether I choose to blacken just the pattern lines or the entire back of the pattern for tracing depends on the softness or hardness of the wood surface, the size of the pattern, and the number of detail lines I want to transfer from the pattern. I also try to make sure that the method I choose both transfers the pattern lines and avoids transferring excess graphite since I know that pencil graphite when burned can become permanently set into the pattern and no amount of erasing will remove it.

For small patterns, I most often will cover the entire back of the tracing pattern with pencil and then use a pen to transfer the pattern to the board by tracing over the design lines. For large patterns or highly detailed patterns, I do take the time to trace along only the pattern lines on the back of the pattern paper. It takes me much less time to trace along individual lines than to clean up the excess graphite caused by rubbing the entire back of the paper on very large patterns.

Some woods accept the graphite better than others. Rubbing the tracing onto the wood is excellent for basswood and creates strong pattern lines. Birch is a harder wood and does not accept rubbing quite as well. For birch, I will use a pen or pencil and individually trace over each design line to achieve a strong pattern transfer. You can do a test tracing either on a scrap piece of wood of the same species that you will be burning or on the back of your project wood to determine which method will work best for your patterns and your wood.

Figure 1.25. Secure the tracing, pencil markings down, to the board. Rub over the pattern lines to force the graphite onto the wood.

Figure 1.26. Leave several pieces of tape in place when you check how successfully the pattern has transferred. Replace the paper and re-rub any light areas.

Figure 1.27. For small projects, coat the entire back surface of the pattern paper with a soft pencil. Use a pen to trace over the pattern lines, tracing a layer of graphite onto the board.

Finishing Steps for Woodburning

Careful consideration of what finish to apply to your final piece is essential. You want the burned texture to show through the finish, not be covered up by it. Following are several finishing techniques that I use frequently because they result in exquisite finished woodburnings.

Sanding and erasing the finished burning

When your woodburning steps are completed, you will discover that the process of burning has left a fine, but rough texture to your work. If you rub your hand across any burning at this point, you will be able to feel the coarseness of the burned fibers that were raised during the burning process. Using very fine-grit sandpaper, lightly go over the entire work to remove this roughness. For this step, I use the foam-core emery boards in my tool kit. They can be laid flat against the wood board and gently moved across the wood without disturbing the burned design. Foam-core emery boards come in a variety of grits. They are readily available at your local drug store and are inexpensive.

After the emery board, I use a white artist's eraser on the entire woodburned design. This removes any remaining pattern lines and guidelines from the work. Use a lint-free cloth or large drafter's dusting brush to remove the eraser rubbings and the sanding dust.

Adding color to your project

Once you have sanded the project and erased any pencil lines, you can add coloring over your work. Any coloring should be done before the final finishing coats of oil or polyurethane are applied. There are three different coloring agents that can be used: colored pencils, watercolors, and oil paints. Each has its own specific advantages.

Colored pencils work best when the woodburning has tight, intriguing details for coloring. The sharp point of the pencil easily fits into any area, no matter how small.

Figure 1.28. *Mallard Drake* was burned on a piece of white birch plywood that was extremely clear in grain, providing a clean background for the application of color.

Watercolors are favored for softer woods such as basswood, butternut, and pine when you want strong but clear colors. Since they are totally transparent, watercolors will color an area of burning without clouding the woodburning strokes.

On harder wood projects, such as those created on birch plywood, where you want that same strong, clear coloring, choose **oil paints**. The oil in these paints will penetrate the fibers of harder woods, whereas watercolors would float on top of the wood surface.

Colored Pencils

Mallard Drake was colored using artist-quality colored pencils (see **Figure 1.28**). For the best coloring effects, keep your pencils very sharp and develop each color slowly in thin, light layers. Because artist-quality colored pencils are semi-transparent, you can add layers of different colors, one over another, to create new hues and tones. Do not force the pencil tip into the burned crevices of the work; instead, keep the pressure gentle. This allows the high areas of the work to become colored while the shading tones of the burning show through the hues.

Any errors or mistakes in your pencil work can be corrected using a white artist's eraser. Transparent tape can also be used to lift a color mistake. Lay the tape over the area that you want to lift; then, using a graphite pencil or an ink pen, gently rub directly on the tape over the error. When you lift off the tape, you will also lift off the pencil color.

Once you have the coloring in place, give your project several light coats of spray polyurethane. This will protect your wood surface as well as seal the colored pencil.

Watercolors

Watercolors are also favorite coloring agents for woodburners. *Old-Timer Fireman* was colored using watercolors (see **Figure 1.29**). These paints are transparent, allowing the woodburning shadows to show through the coloring. Woods such as basswood, butternut, and pine take watercolors excellently. Because soft woods are extremely porous, the water in the watercolors is pulled deeply into the wood fibers, taking the coloring agent with it. This deep penetration of the color gives you a rich, vibrant finish.

Place a small amount of each of your watercolors on a clean tile, and then add several drops of water to thin the paint. By keeping the early stages of coloring very thin, you can develop the color slowly by adding more layers of paint. Watercolors can be either mixed together on the tile to create new color shades or laid one color over another on the burning for new hues and tones. Allow each coating of watercolors to dry well before adding more color to that area.

When the painting is completed, allow the woodburning to dry overnight. Then, apply several light coats of polyurethane spray to the entire project to protect the wood and watercolors.

If *Old-Timer Fireman* had been woodburned onto a hard wood such as birch, oil paints would have been used for the coloring and should have given the exact same effect as the watercolors shown in the sample.

Figure 1.29. *Old-Timer Fireman* was colored with watercolor paints. The watercolors are transparent, allowing the burn lines to show through.

Oil Paints

As I mentioned earlier, hard woods, such as birch plywood, take artist oil paints very well. Here, the oil base of the paint penetrates the wood fibers, allowing the coloring agent to be set deeply into the wood surface.

Place a small amount of your oil paint on a clean palette. In a small container, mix one part sunflower or linseed oil with one part turpentine. Use this mixture to thin your oil paints until they are transparent. Thin layers can now be applied over your woodburning, slowly building up the color tone (see **Figure 1.30**). Oil paint is an excellent medium to use when you need gradually blended color changes. Allow each layer of oil paint work to dry well before adding a new layer. For large areas of color, this can take from one hour to several days, depending on the wood species and color application.

When the coloring is completed, allow the project to dry well. Again, this can take several days or more. Then, apply your finishing coats of polyurethane spray sealer.

Figure 1.30. Oil paints are transparent colors that allow the full depth of the woodburned tones to show. For the *American Eagle*, titanium white oil paint was added to the tips of the feathers to create a contrast to the black-brown color of the woodburning.

Sealing the wood project

Woodburnings should be sealed once the pattern work and any coloring is completed. This protects the burning work and seals the wood from dirt and oils. There are several ways you can seal your project.

Spray polyurethane is a quick and easy way to seal any woodburning that has been colored, no matter what color medium you have used—colored pencils, oil paints, or watercolors. Because the sealer is applied through an aerosol spray, it does not disturb or move your color work with brush strokes. You can obtain high gloss, gloss, and semi-matte formulas. Build up your finish in light layers, allowing each layer to dry thoroughly before adding the next. Polyurethane also comes in a liquid version that is applied with a soft, clean brush. Follow the directions on the can for application. As with the spray, several light coats work best.

Oil finishes give a durable finish to any woodburning work and bring out the natural grain in wood. Tung oil and Danish oil finish are two common types of oil finishes. Follow the directions on the can or jar. Most oils are applied by brushing one coat of oil finish on the entire project. Allow that coat to set for ten to fifteen minutes; then, with a clean lint-free cloth, wipe the excess oil from the wood. Allow this coating to dry overnight, and then apply a second coat in the same manner.

Paste floor wax is a third type of finish that you can give your woodburning projects (see **Figure 1.31**). As with the other types of finishes, follow the manufacturer's directions. With a clean lint-free cloth, rub one light coat of paste wax on the entire piece. Allow this coating to dry for several minutes. When it starts to dry to a cloudy appearance, use a new clean, soft cloth to rub the polish, buffing it to a soft sheen. Several coats of paste wax can be applied. If you apply too much paste wax and your project has a milky look to it, scrub the milky areas vigorously with an old toothbrush to rub off the extra paste wax.

Figure 1.31. Even though woodburning is permanent and weatherproof, the project surface will need to be sealed. Polyurethane, paste wax, and Danish oil are all excellent sealers for either wood or gourd projects.

Part 2

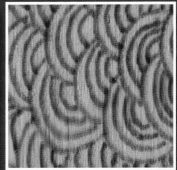

Practice

That old adage about practice makes perfect is true. Before you start any woodburning project, you'll want to practice on a piece of scrap wood. In this chapter, we'll discuss the basic techniques of woodburning, like how to create light and dark tones and how to create texture. Then, I'll show you how to create a practice board and give you some exercises so you can hone your skills before you start your project. When you are comfortable with the techniques, we will delve into the theory behind woodburning to discuss tonal values and other ideas that will help you perfect your art.

Using Shading and Texture

The comment I hear the most from people viewing a woodburning is, "Look at all that shading." The shading they are referring to comes from a variety of techniques. In this section, let's take a look at the basic woodburning techniques and how they are applied to create shading.

Creating light and dark tones

As you work any woodburning pattern, you will want to create light, medium, and dark areas within the design. These different tones, or tonal values, are what give depth to the finished image. Several ingredients go into creating the differences between the dark areas and the light

One-Temperature Tool　　　**Variable-Temperature Tool**

Figure 2.1. Here is a practice board for creating the tonal values discussed throughout this section. The two left columns were burned using a one-temperature tool. The universal tip was used for rows one through three and row five. The right two columns were burned using a variable-temperature tool. Rows one through three and row five were created using the writing tip.

Row 1: Temperature of the Tip. These tonal value changes were created by controlling the temperature of the tool tip.

Row 2: Burning Time. Pale tones can be burned by moving the tool tip quickly across the wood surface. Slow movement darkens the tonal coloring of the burn.

Row 3: Layers of Strokes. The more layers of burned lines or strokes that you apply to an area, the darker in tonal value that area will become.

Row 4: Type of Tip. Fine point tools burn darker lines than wide, flat tool tips. The fine point tip (left) and the ballpoint tip (right) were used for the one-temperature tool side of this chart. The small round tip (left) and the large shader tip (right) were used for the variable-temperature tool side.

Row 5: Style of Stroke. The type of stroke that you choose and the density in which you pack that stroke also can be used to develop tonal values.

areas of a woodburning: temperature of the tool tip, length of time in making the stroke, layering of the strokes, type of tool you use, and type of stroke you use. With practice, these techniques can easily be learned by the beginning wood-burner and used to create wonderfully detailed tonal value burnings. All of the exercises in this section can be done with either a variable-temperature tool or a one-temperature tool.

Temperature of the Tip

First, let's look at the temperature of the tool tip. Low temperatures create light-colored burnings. As you increase the temperature setting on your woodburning tool, the lines gradually become darker (see **Figure 2.1, row 1**). As a general rule, begin your burnings on the lowest setting possible. This allows you time to discover the particular properties of the wood on which you are working. Remember that each piece of wood will burn at a different rate, different color, and different depth. A low temperature in the early stages of your project will also allow you to slowly develop and establish the basic light and dark areas of the design. You can then deepen the different areas to create sharp contrast in the work.

Practice: Let's take a few moments to try out this technique. Find a piece of extra wood, prefer-

ably the same wood that you will use for your first burnings. By using the same wood for practice as you would for an actual piece, you can see how the burning looks on that particular wood and how the wood's characteristics will affect the finished project.

First, set up your work area and find the most comfortable way to hold your woodburning pen. If you are using a one-temperature tool, hold it in the handgrip area as if you were holding a pen or pencil (see **Figure 2.2**). You can use your second hand to support the hand that's holding the pen. For the variable-temperature tool, simply hold the pen in the foam grip area as you would any writing tool (see **Figure 2.3**).

Then, turn on your woodburning tool. If you are using a one-temperature tool, begin burning right away to achieve pale values. As the tool heats up, you will have darker values (see **Figure 2.4**). If you are using a variable-temperature tool, set the heat to a low setting and burn a few lines. Then, move to the next higher setting and burn a few more lines (see **Figure 2.5**). Continue this process until you have burned with several of the different settings. For more practice with this technique, be sure to see Light and Dark Exercise One in the Patterns for Practice section on page 52.

Figure 2.3. Hold the pen in the foam grip area as you would any writing tool. Because the tips of variable-temperature pens are much shorter than those of one-temperature tools, your hand is closer to the woodburning surface.

Figure 2.4. Practice burning strokes in different temperatures. I'm using the universal tip on its side and pulling the tool to create broad, burned strokes. The lower lines in this section were done while the tool was heating; the top line was worked at full temperature.

Figure 2.2. Hold the one-temperature tool like a pen or pencil. I am using my second hand as a rest and support for my working hand. This provides me with the added height to keep the tool tip on its sharp working edge. The wide heat shield below the rubber handgrip area keeps your fingertips away from the hot burning tip. To burn fine lines as I am doing here, hold the tool in a comfortable upright position.

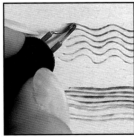

Figure 2.5. Here, I'm using the variable-temperature tool to change temperature. The bottom lines of each set were burned at a low temperature; the top lines were burned at a higher temperature.

Conducting Burn Tests

Once you've practiced with temperature, perform this test to record what your burner is capable of with different types of material. Remember that, for one-temperature tools, your temperature variations come during the time that your tool heats to its top setting. Lines burned soon after you plug in your one-temperature tool will be paler in tonal value than those burned after the tool reaches its full heat setting. Variable-temperature tools can, of course, be adjusted to low, medium, or high heats with the thermostat unit. Set the variable-temperature tool on each marked setting, and burn a line or a small square of a texture pattern into your test board. With a pencil, mark which number setting was used for that line. When you have worked through the range of settings, decide which will be best for your work.

As an example, with my particular variable-temperature tool with a setting range of 1 through 10 and working on birch plywood, I have found that a setting of 4 is my low (or cool) range, 5 is my middle (or medium) range, and 6 is my high (or hot) range. Any settings below 4 are too cool to change the color of the birch during a burning. Those above 6 are far too hot. (Of course, these settings only work for birch plywood. Different settings would be needed if I used a different wood.)

Test the temperature ranges available on your burner and note which settings are best for your working style. Remember, your settings will change depending on the material you are burning. (Fill in your number settings on the charts to the right. I've provided basswood, poplar plywood, and birch plywood as materials, but feel free to change these to match the material you're using.)

My example settings for birch plywood are:	
Below 4	too cool to use
4	low or cool burns
4½	medium-low burns
5	medium burns
5½	medium-high burns
6	high or hot burns
Above 6	too hot to use

My temperature settings for basswood are:	
	too cool to use
	low or cool burns
	medium-low burns
	medium burns
	medium-high burns
	high or hot burns
	too hot to use

My temperature settings for popular plywood are:	
	too cool to use
	low or cool burns
	medium-low burns
	medium burns
	medium-high burns
	high or hot burns
	too hot to use

My temperature settings for birch plywood are:	
	too cool to use
	low or cool burns
	medium-low burns
	medium burns
	medium-high burns
	high or hot burns
	too hot to use

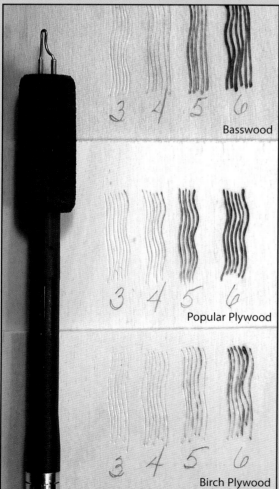

Basswood

Popular Plywood

Birch Plywood

This temperature test was done with a variable-temperature tool ranging from a setting of 3 through 6 on a scale with 10 as the highest temperature possible for my burning unit. The top sample board is basswood, the center board is popular plywood, and the bottom board is birch plywood. You can see that each wood burns differently at the same temperature settings.

Burning Time

The second method for creating light and dark areas in a woodburning is the length of time during which the tool touches any given area. The longer you allow the tool to touch one specific point on the wood, the darker the tool will burn. Quick strokes create light burnings; slow strokes develop dark burn lines (see **Figure 2.1, row 2**).

Practice: To practice changing the speed of your tool tip, use the same board that you did for the tool temperature practice. Move the tool tip across the surface slowly to create some dark strokes; move the tool tip quickly for others (see **Figure 2.6**). You can also try to vary the tool speed in the middle of the stroke to get a gradual change in tone. For more practice with this technique, be sure to see Light and Dark Exercise Two in the Patterns for Practice section on page 54.

Layers of Strokes

The third way to create light and dark areas is to layer your burned strokes. Generally, the more layers of texture strokes you apply to one area, the darker that area becomes (see **Figure 2.1, row 3**). Repeated layering of strokes creates dense, thick areas of burning, covering more and more of the original wood background.

Please note here that I have not mentioned pressure. Finely worked woodburning is done by allowing the tool to rest on the wood surface, not by forcing the tool into the wood surface. You should glide your tool across your project using only the pressure that you would normally use when writing with a pencil or pen. Forcing or pushing the tool tip into the wood creates halos around your texture lines so you end up with a deeply burned line, but the surrounding areas also have been scorched to a medium shade. If you find yourself forcing the tool tip, stop your burning and return to a light writing pressure.

Figure 2.6. In the top photo, the upper lines were made by moving the tool across the surface quickly. The bottom lines were burned moving the tool across the surface slowly, making very dark, black-brown lines. The inset shows the same effect with a wire-tip tool—the upper lines were created by moving the tool slowly and the lower lines by moving the tool quickly.

It should also be noted here that turning up the temperature on your variable-temperature tool or using your one-temperature tool at full heat will create darker tones of sepia very quickly. However, hot tools can cause bleeding or haloing. A very hot tool tip will burn the area that it touches to a very dark brown or black brown coloring, but it can also scorch the area surrounding the tool tip. This scorching will give a halo of light to medium brown beyond the section that you want burned. By working with a lower heat setting and building your dark tonal values in layers, you avoid bleeding and haloing problems.

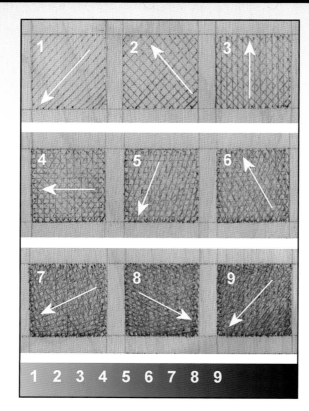

Figure 2.7. Practice working in layers. You can see nine gradients of chocolate-toned woodburning. These different shades of chocolate were created by adding layer upon layer of woodburning until the exact color tone was achieved.

In **Figure 2.7**, I worked by burning layer upon layer of straight lines. With each new layer, the direction of the line was changed. There are nine distinct shades ranging from very pale to medium-dark. Compare the burnings to the sepia brown value strip and you can see that there are still many shades toward the black that can be worked. This series of brown colors from pale tan through black brown is called a sepia scale, sepia meaning variations of brown.

Because this is the most common method of developing tonal values in a woodburning and because of the wide range of different values you can create, we will look at the steps needed to burn your own tonal value sepia scale. As you

Figure 2.8. The narrow loop of this tip creates very dark scale-shaped marks when touched to the wood surface.

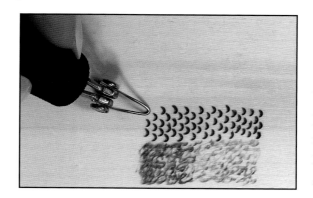

work through this exercise, notice that the tonal value is controlled by the number of layers of burning you use within one square. At no time during this exercise is the temperature of the tool increased to create darker colors. Adding layers of burned lines to an area gives you far greater control over the final color depth of that area than turning the temperature of your tool to a higher heat setting.

Practice: First, set your tool at a low-medium temperature. Then, use a soft #2 pencil and a T-square, ruler, or straightedge to create nine one-inch squares on a board of your choice. Leave one-quarter inch of space between each square.

Burn the square with tightly spaced diagonal lines all running in the same direction. In your same square, burn a second set of lines going in the opposite direction. Your sample should now look like the second square.

Next, burn a third set of lines running vertically in the area. Your burning should now look like the third square. Continue adding lines until you have nine layers of lines. Compare your burning with each of the squares as you burn.

Notice in all of the sample squares that the coloring is very even throughout the square. Because each new layer was laid down in a different direction than the previous work, the burning takes on a very even appearance throughout the worked area. Any small imperfections in one layer of burning are balanced out in the later layers. By using layers of woodburning at a low-medium temperature, you have total control over both the final color shade of any area in your project and the evenness of that color work. For more practice with this technique, see Light and Dark Exercise Three in the Patterns for Practice section on page 58.

Type of Tip

Your choice of tool tips also determines the burned value of an area. Wide-faced tips do not reach as high a temperature as fine- or narrow-faced tips because the heat is dispersed across a larger surface area on the tip's face. Therefore, a wide-faced tip will often give a lighter burned color than a narrow tip (see **Figure 2.1, row 4**).

Practice: Experiment with the different types of tips. You can use the same board that you did for the other practice sections. Try touching fine tips to the wood to create darker impressions (see **Figure 2.8**). If you have a tip with a broad, flat surface, practice pulling it across the wood to make a softer, lighter mark (see **Figure 2.9**). You'll also want to try using the sides of your tool tips to see the types of marks they make. Continue working to become comfortable with capabilities of the different tips.

Figure 2.9. The large shading tip of the one-temperature tool is often leaf- or triangle-shaped. The broad, flat area of the tool burns medium tones in large areas without leaving individual lines.

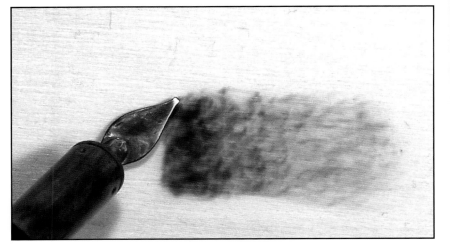

One-Temperature Tool Techniques

We've touched on a number of techniques in the book. Remember to keep these principles in mind as you woodburn. These simple tips will increase your success.

1. **Keep your tool extremely clean.** As you work, take frequent breaks from the woodburning to remove any carbon build-up from the brass tip. Carbon build-up not only causes uneven burning, but also leaves behind a small amount of black deposit in the burned line. Clean, light-toned lines come from clean tips.

2. **Pay special attention to the very pale areas of any project.** Mark these on your pattern to remember where those pale tones will be. When you plug in your tool, either to start a burning session or after cleaning a tip, it will begin heating. This is the time to burn the pale tones. As the tool reaches its hot temperature setting, move on to the darker areas of the work.

3. **Use certain texture strokes to ensure pale tonal values.** Crosshatching is a favorite because it allows an equal amount of original wood coloring in the texture to balance out the burned lines. By adding more layers to the crosshatched texture, you can slowly develop the mid-tone values. Widely spaced curved-line texturing is another excellent burning stroke for the one-temperature tool.

4. **Apply a light pressure as you work.** The tool tip should slide or glide across the surface. Light pressure allows the sharp edge of the tool to do the burning work; heavier pressure pushes the tip deep into the wood, causing both the tip and the tip's sides to burn the wood.

Figure 2.10. A fine tip, like this ballpoint tip for the one-temperature tool, can be used to create tightly packed, dark spots for deep-toned areas in your work. With a simple touch-then-lift motion, this tip will quickly fill an area with black-brown toned circles of burning.

Style of Stroke

The style of stroke pattern that you use in any given area of your picture gives interest to each area of your work. A lightly burned swirl pattern of curls will give a soft, light coloring that is excellent for shading. Because the curls allow large amounts of the original wood coloring to show through the work, these areas will appear light. In contrast, if you just touch the tip of your tool to the wood to burn a small, tightly packed dot pattern, you can achieve extremely dark areas.

Practice: Again, use the same board that you used for the other practice sections. Begin by choosing a fine tip. First practice creating small, tightly packed dots for a dark area (see **Figure 2.10**). Then, using the same tip, make curls to achieve an area that's lighter in tone (see **Figure 2.11**). We'll work more with this technique throughout the next section, Creating a Practice Board, on page 40. For even more practice with this technique, be sure to see Light and Dark Exercise Four in the Patterns for Practice section on page 60.

Creating texture strokes

In addition to light, medium, and dark areas within a design, you'll also want to have different visual textures within a design. The type of stroke, or texture, you choose for burning a particular part of your work will often depend on the appearance you want to create. For example, a blade of grass close to the viewer would need a stroke that is created with a smooth, flowing line, but a tree in the background might have a tight random curl to mimic the look of leaves and the tree's trunk might have a short dash stroke to imply bark. By using a variety of visual texture, or stroke, patterns within one woodburned design, you add visual interest to each area and element of the burning. We'll look at the huge variety of visual textures you can create in more detail when we get to the practice board on page 41.

Physical, or Actual, Texture

As you create your own sample board, you will notice that some burned lines and visual textures will have actual, physical texture. Low-temperature burnings scorch the surface of the wood. These low settings are enough to change the wood coloring without actually burning a trough or groove into the wood fibers. As your woodburning tool tip, whether a one-temperature tool or a variable-temperature tool, begins to reach the medium to medium-high settings, the fibers of the wood do burn, which creates a groove. Very high temperature settings will burn deep troughs or deep craters down into your project's surface. These grooves, troughs, and craters add actual, physical texture to the work. Adding physical texture through the use of medium to high temperature settings adds interest to the final work.

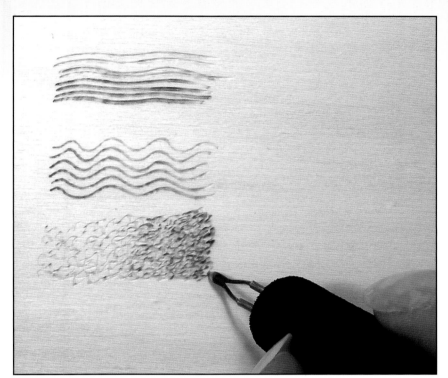

Figure 2.11. The same fine tip can be used to create a pattern of curls for a lighter area of tone. I used a small round tip for the variable-temperature tool to show how this can be done with either type of tool.

However, since low-temperature burnings do not create physical texture in the work, the tonal value techniques taught in this book do not depend on actual physical texture; they instead focus on visual texture, patterns, strokes, and layering.

Variable-Temperature Tool Techniques

Remember to keep these tips in mind to aid you in using the variable-temperature tool to your best advantage.

1. **Mark your setting numbers in pencil directly on the wood.** After you have practiced with your variable-temperature burner to discover the color tones that can be created with each temperature, use a pencil to mark that setting number on or near the corresponding tonal value on your tracing. The pencil numbers on your project will remind you as you work which temperature setting you wish to use.

2. **Densely packed line textures can be created in light or dark tones.** Because you have more control over the temperature, you also have more control over the darkness or paleness of the color tone. By using a low setting, dense textures can be created so that little of the unburned wood shows, yet the sepia, or brown, tone is extremely pale in value.

3. **Develop your tonal values slowly through layers, not through heat.** Just because you can turn a variable-temperature tool on its highest setting for very dark areas does not mean that quick, hot burnings are always the best for black areas in your design. There are many tones of color possible between dark brown and black. By developing the burning slowly through layers, you can choose which tone works best for each area.

4. **Keep your tips extremely clean.** Develop the habit of cleaning and polishing the tips often and thoroughly to ensure the best quality of line possible.

Creating a Practice Board

One of the fun ways to learn to control your wood-burning strokes is to create a practice board. This gives you a working surface on which to experiment with the wide variety of strokes that you will use. It can also be used to record any new strokes and layering techniques that you discover as you grow in this craft. Plus, because this board is only used as practice, it's a great place to work until you learn to control your strokes. Once you have control over the stroke, you can move to your working project with confidence.

I also use my practice board to work out textures and specific elements of a pattern. Small pattern samples not only let me create the textures that I want to use but also help me establish the lights and darks in a pattern before I start on my actual project.

My practice board is a 12" wide by 20" high piece of birch plywood since this is the wood species that I use the most (see **Figure 2.12**). You may wish to

make your practice board on your favorite wood surface so that your practice work will show you the same burns as those on your finished projects.

Begin by creating a pencil-line grid on the wood. I used a soft #2 pencil and the T-square to section my board into one-inch squares with one-quarter-inch spacing between each square. As you begin each new project or approach a texture that you have not done before, try it out first on your practice board. Number each square with a pencil so that you may keep a corresponding card file for each square that notes the particular tool tip you used, the temperature settings for the burner, and on which project you used that texture.

Keep your practice board close to your work area. This makes it quick and easy to add new textures, and it will be handy for choosing previously tested textures for a new project.

Quick Reference Texture Chart

Square #	Texture Name	Tonal Value
Squares 1–5	Dash Stroke	pale to dark tones
Squares 6–14	Linear Circles	pale value to dark tones
Squares 15–23	Wide-Spaced Crosshatch	medium to black tones
Squares 24–32	Tight-Spaced Crosshatch	medium to black tones
Squares 33–37	Random Curls	pale to dark tones
Square 38	Check Marks	medium to dark tone
Square 39	Wide-Spaced Zigzag	medium tone
Square 40	Random Zigzag	medium tone
Square 41	Sun Rays or Grass Strokes	medium tone
Square 42	Wavy Lines	medium to dark tone
Square 43	Seashell Circles	dark tones
Square 44	Tightly Packed Zigzag	medium tone
Square 45	Tight Circles	medium to dark tone
Square 46	ABC	dark tone
Square 47	568	dark tone
Sqaure 48	Scales	dark tone
Square 49	SUE	medium to dark tone
Square 50	Mountain Peaks	dark tone
Square 51	Quilting	medium tone
Square 52	Overlapping Hearts	medium tone
Square 53	Herringbone	medium to dark tone
Square 54	Diagonal Ripples	medium to dark tone

Square #	Texture Name	Tonal Value
Square 55	Water Ripples	medium to dark tone
Square 56	Tightly Packed Spots	dark to black tone
Square 57	Long Scales	dark to black tone
Square 58	Close-up Branches and Leaves	medium to black tones
Square 59	Wood Grain	pale to dark tones
Square 60	Tall Grass Clumps	medium to dark tones
Squares 61–64	Scrubby Lines	pale to dark tones
Square 65	Small Crosshatched Elements	pale to dark tones
Squares 66–68	Straight Lines	pale to dark tones
Square 69	Long Curved Line	pale to dark tones
Square 70	Short Curved Line	pale to dark tones
Square 71	Veining Curved Line	pale to dark tones
Square 72	Background Trees	medium to dark tones
Square 73	Tall Grass	pale to dark tones
Square 74	Stone Walkway	medium tones
Square 75	Evergreens	pale to dark tones
Square 76	Deciduous Trees	pale to dark tones
Square 77	Pines and Deciduous Shrubs	pale to dark tones
Square 78	Roof and Shadows	pale to dark tones
Square 79	Barn Boards	pale to dark tones
Square 80	Bricks	pale to dark tones
Square 81	Small Pine and Shrub	pale to dark tones

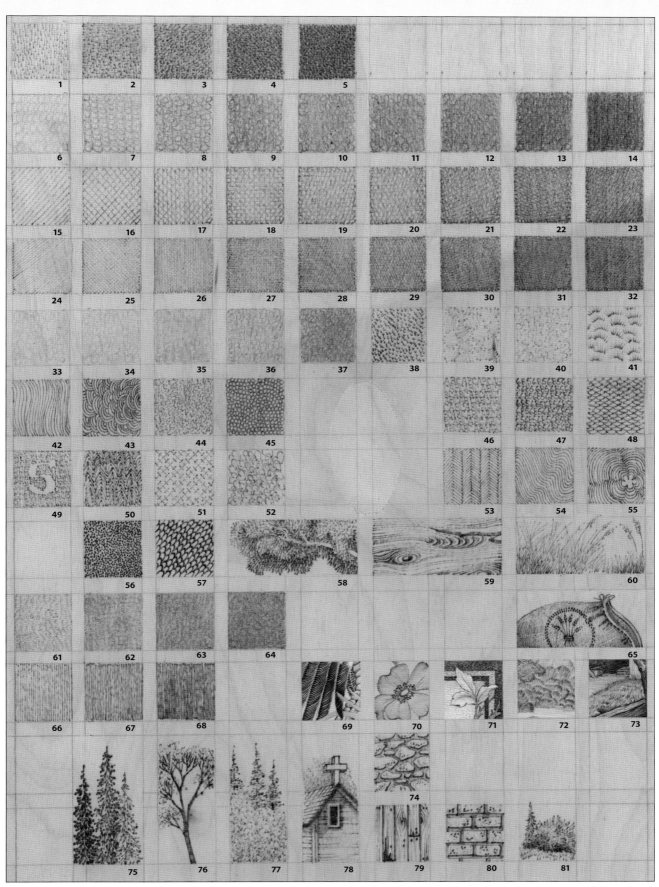

Figure 2.12. By creating a practice board that you keep close to your work area, you can test new textures, tonal values, and even small pieces of a design before you begin work on your project surface.

Tonal value, or sepia scale value, textures

There are a variety of textures that lend themselves extremely well to realistic shading in a woodburning. This series of textures can be developed into darker tones by repeating the texture in layers. With each new layer, change the direction in which the texture is burned. Notice the top four rows of work on the practice board (**Squares 1–32**): They slowly move through gradient tones of chocolate. Each of these rows has been created using a different texturing stroke. That particular stroke was then repeated through each square of the row, adding more tonal depth to each subsequent block (see **Figure 2.13**). A low-medium temperature was used to create these samples; the temperature was not changed during the work.

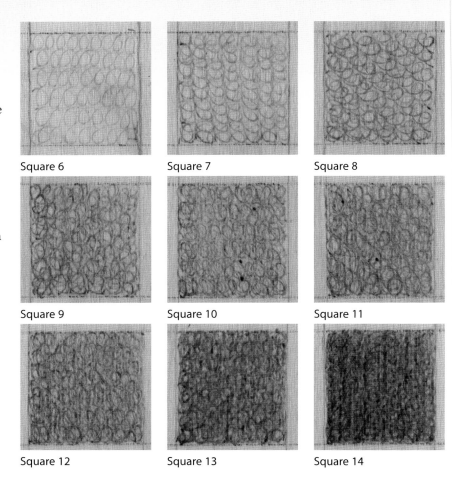

Square 6   Square 7   Square 8

Square 9   Square 10   Square 11

Square 12   Square 13   Square 14

Figure 2.13. In this section, we will examine the practice of layering textures. By adding light layers of texture, you can slowly build up the tonal values of your design. By rotating the texture on each application, the area will become gradually darker. Squares 6 to 14 show just one example of this technique.

Dash Stroke

This sample was created using a short dashlike stroke and the small round tip (see **Figure 2.14**). The first square (**Square 1**) shows the texturing running in a vertical pattern. The second square (**Square 2**) was first worked vertically, and then another layer of burning was added running horizontally. A third layer of burning appears in the last square (**Square 3**); this one runs diagonally across the first two layers. The early stages of this texture have a light dappling of darker spots, but, as you add more layers, this will disappear. This is an excellent pattern for small areas that need to be a dark tonal value.

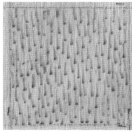 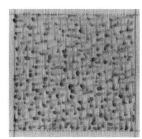 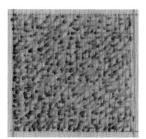

Square 1   Square 2   Square 3

Figure 2.14. Dash stroke.

Linear Circles

Very small circles make up this texturing (see **Figure 2.15**). Begin at the top of the square to make your first circle. Allow the tool tip to flow into the next circle, then the next. You are burning a row of connected circles that run from left to right across the square (**Square 6**). A second layer of connected circles running from top to bottom is added to the second square (**Square 7**). In the third square (**Square 8**), use a diagonal direction for the third layer. This pattern is great to use to fill in an area that has already been detailed with a high-temperature outlining.

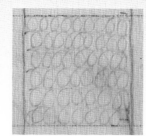
Square 6

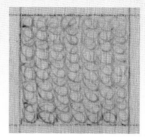
Square 7

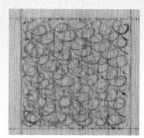
Square 8

Figure 2.15. Linear circles.

Wide-Spaced Crosshatch

Created with widely spaced straight lines, crosshatching is a classic texture used in pen and ink studies (see **Figure 2.16**). The first two layers (**Squares 15** and **16**) are worked on the diagonal, the third (**Square 17**) on the vertical, and the fourth (**Square 18**) runs horizontal to the design. Because of the wide spacing, the burn lines of each layer can be seen once the tonal value has been developed. This adds interest to the shaded areas because of the visual tension caused by the changing line directions.

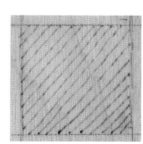
Square 15

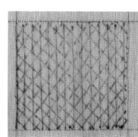
Square 16

Square 17

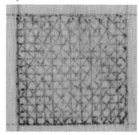
Square 18

Figure 2.16. Wide-spaced crosshatch.

Tight-Spaced Crosshatch

By packing the straight lines tightly during each layer of work, this version of crosshatching is excellent for very realistic designs (see **Figure 2.17**). Unlike wide-spaced work, this texture quickly loses the linear effect as the diagonal, vertical, and horizontal lines are added (**Squares 24–27**). Tight-spaced crosshatching is an excellent choice when you need perfect control in the work.

Square 24

Square 25

Square 26

Figure 2.17. Tight-spaced crosshatch.

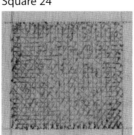
Square 27

Random Curls

Creating random curls is really nothing more than doodling loops with the tool tip (see **Figure 2.18**). Place the tip of the tool onto the wood and start creating very small, tightly packed circular shapes (**Square 33**). Do not lift your tip as you work; instead, flow right into the next curl. Because the tool tip remains in contact with the wood throughout the burning of that layer, there are no dark spots created as happens with a start-and-stop stroke. Random curls texturing creates a very soft texture when used in light layers (**Squares 34–35**) and is perfect for working over high-temperature outlines and details.

Square 33

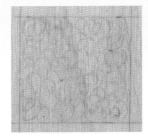
Square 34

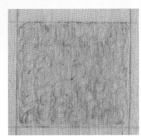
Square 35

Figure 2.18. Random curls.

Scrubby Lines

This style of texturing is also random and chaotic and worked as if you were scrubbing the wood-burned color onto the wood, moving in whatever direction is necessary to completely fill an area (see **Figure 2.19**). Place the tool tip onto the board, and do not lift the tip as you work to create tightly packed, zigzag-type lines (**Square 61**). The zigzags are very short, not much more than ⅛" long. You can see in the sample that they are laid down in a random pattern; no attempt is made to keep each zigzag the exact same length. The early stages of this texture will have that dark spot, dappled effect. However, thicker layering will create very dark chocolate values (**Squares 62 and 63**). This is an excellent texture to use when you need black tones in your work.

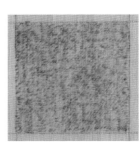
Square 61

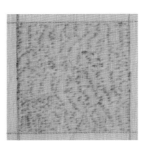
Square 62

Square 63

Figure 2.19. Scrubby lines.

Repeating pattern textures

Not every woodburning needs careful, controlled shading to create realistic images. Many designs can be approached using fun little patterns within the design as the shading work. Anything that you can conceive can work as a texturing pattern. Take a look at the following examples.

Check Marks and Zigzags

Check marks in a random order are wonderful marks to create texture (see **Figure 2.20**). **Square 38** is created using little check marks. Because the texture is very small, even at a low temperature this check mark will take on a medium to dark tone. A nice contrast is created because of this dark tone against the pale color of the wood.

Quick back-and-forth strokes create a zigzag pattern, or texture, to the burned area. The texture in **Square 39** is a wide-spaced, chaotic zigzag pattern. This is a great pattern for working large areas of tree leaves.

Square 40 has a random-moving zigzag texture. Place your tool tip onto the board and do not lift it. As you work the texture, just keep changing directions. This will fill your working area with a dark to light variegated line.

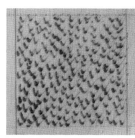  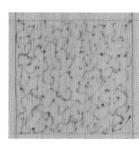

Square 38　　　　Square 39　　　　Square 40

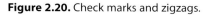

Figure 2.20. Check marks and zigzags.

By tightly packing a random zigzag stroke (**Square 44**), you can create wonderful mid-tone colors. As you work to constantly change the direction of the zigzag, let one part of the line touch or cross over another.

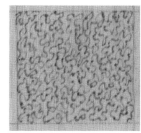

Square 44

Wavy Lines and Sea Shell Circles

Try wavy lines as another way to texture your work (see **Figure 2.21**). The first square to the left (**Square 42**) is made up of wavy lines. Begin by pulling one line into the work area. Let that line move gracefully back and forth through the space. Lay a second line next to the first, following the path the first line created. Continue until your area is completely filled. As you work, do not try to be exact with each line; let the overall texture change to create new movement.

In the middle (**Square 43**) is a classic oriental-styled pattern of seashell circles. On one edge of your area, create a very small half circle. Another half circle, just a littler larger, is made, surrounding this first one. About four to five half circles create one seashell. The next seashell is worked against the outermost half circle of the first.

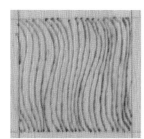 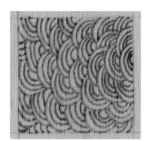

Square 42　　　　Square 43

Figure 2.21. Wavy lines.

Letters and Numbers

Numbers, letters, and even well-recognized symbols can be used to create a texture pattern (see **Figure 2.22**). In this left square (**Square 49**), three letters—*S, U,* and *E*—have been used, creating the name *SUE* as background texture.

In **Figure 2.23**, the left and middle squares (**Squares 46** and **47**) were test samples for the *My Room Gingerbread Man*, pattern on page 112. The first square (Square 46) is made up of the ABCs, and the second (Square 47) with 5, 6, and 8. Notice that I left out the number 7. That is because 5, 6, and 8 all have a circular pattern, whereas 7 is a linear design. Not only letters, but also entire writings or quotes can create fantastic background textures. In the *American Eagle* pattern, see page 146, a letter from a Civil War general could be used to fill in the background space. The writing, therefore, makes the background as important as the foreground image of the eagle.

Square 49

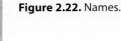

Figure 2.22. Names.

Square 46

Square 47

Figure 2.23. Letters and numbers.

Mountain Peaks

Small, interconnected mountain peaks are worked in **Figure 2.24** (**Square 50**). The sides of each peak are slightly curved because this keeps the texture from becoming too rigid. First, one row of peaks was created. The next row was then laid under the first, with the second-row peaks being tucked into the first.

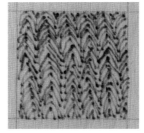

Square 50

Figure 2.24. Mountain peaks.

Quilting

Figure 2.25 (**Square 51**) is a broken crosshatch pattern that gives the impression of quilting stitches. A very widely spaced crosshatch is first applied on the diagonal. The second layer of crosshatch is made up of dashed lines, which creates the small crosses in the previous layer and allows a small area of original wood to show.

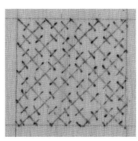

Square 51

Figure 2.25. Quilting.

Scales

Fish scales, or dragon scales, were created for **Figure 2.26**. This is a design made up of small semi-circle rows (**Square 48**). Notice that any individual curve is not a full half circle but instead a small arch. The next row is applied starting the semi-circles in the middle, or at the high point, of the semi-circles in the first row.

Figure 2.26. Scales.

Square 48

Herringbones

A herringbone pattern is wonderful for fun woodburning (see **Figure 2.27**). This pattern is burned in rows of short diagonal strips (**Square 53**). The next row changes the direction of the diagonal. When the area is completely burned, you have rows or stripes, and you also have a zigzag effect to the finished work.

Figure 2.27. Herringbones.

Square 53

Ripples

Ripples do not have to run in the direction of the element or area that is being worked (see **Figure 2.28**). The left square (**Square 54**) obviously has both vertical and horizontal sides, but the ripple pattern was laid down on the diagonal.

A different ripple effect is shown in the right square (**Square 55**). For this sample, a simple shape was first burned. Then, expanding lines of the same pattern were worked out from the first. If, for example, you had a cluster of leaves that had been outlined, you could burn water ripples around that cluster to fill in the surrounding background space.

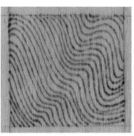 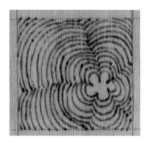

Figure 2.28. Ripples.

Square 54 Square 55

Straight-Line Variations

All three of these squares were created using a straight-line burn (see **Figure 2.29**). The first square (**Square 66**) has one layer of straight lines, the middle square (**Square 67**) has two layers, and the right square (**Square 68**) has three layers. Straight-line fill is great for filling in either small or large areas where you need a dark tone. However, this pattern does not burn evenly. Notice in the third square (Square 68) that the bottom section of the square is darker than the top. The variations in tonal value created by this texture are perfect for the wood bark of a large tree and for ground shadows.

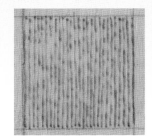 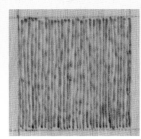 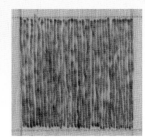

Square 66   Square 67   Square 68

Figure 2.29. Straight lines.

Hearts and Circles

Overlapping or closely spaced hearts and circles also make excellent background fill (see **Figure 2.30**). Small overlapping hearts fill in the space of the top square (**Square 52**). All of the hearts have been laid down in one diagonal direction so that the double loops are to the upper left and the points of the hearts are oriented toward the bottom right. This pattern works very well for fun feathers.

The bottom square (**Square 45**) is filled with tightly packed, tiny circles. Each small circle is touched by the surrounding circles. An area that uses this texture will retain the circular effect, which burns to a medium-dark tone, but it also will leave some of the original wood showing.

Figure 2.30. Hearts and circles.

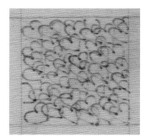

Square 52

Square 45

Tightly Packed Spots and Long Scale Strokes

Some textures create very black areas in woodburning (see **Figure 2.31**). The top square (**Square 56**) is one of these textures. This sample was done by simply touching the tool tip to the wood and then lifting the tip. Each touch burns a very dark spot into the design. Here the spots were worked loosely packed, but had they been allowed to touch, totally filling the square, this burning would appear black-chocolate when completed. This is a fast and easy way to render the dark tones in your work.

Elongated fish scales have been burned in diagonal rows for the bottom square (**Square 57**). Notice how much darker in tonal value this burning is than the previous sample of scales (see Square 48, Figure 2.26). Because the elongated stroke is not as easy flowing as the semi-circle, more time is required to create the elongation. When any textured burning is done in a slow motion, the burning becomes deeper in tonal value.

Figure 2.31. Dark strokes.

Square 56

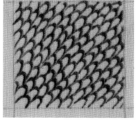

Square 57

Other texturing and shading patterns

Most texture patterns, such as the ones we discussed in the previous sections, are used independent of the shape of the element in which they are used. For example, the scrubby-line stroke, can be used to shade the door of an old car as easily as it can be used to shade the facial features of a stylized sun face. However, some texture strokes and shading strokes are determined by the area that they are to fill. With this grouping of textures, the shading strokes follow the curvature of the element to give it visual movement. The curve of the element is usually determined by its outlines. The scrubby line can be used to add shading to a leaf and will make the leaf darker in the correct areas; however, by using a curved-line stroke that flows with the twisting of that leaf as your shading pattern, you can accentuate the impression that the leaf rolls over and away from the foreground. Following is a group of shading and texturing patterns and samples of their use in some of the finished woodburnings in this book.

Square 69

Long and Short Curved Lines

Curved lines are an excellent texture for shading an area while accenting the area's natural shape (see **Figure 2.32**). The first square (**Square 69**) shows a sample of the long curved line used to create the feather look of *Dragonette*'s wings. Notice that the lines are black along the outer edge of the wing, where they were started, and pale to a dark brown as the strokes are pulled toward the inside edge. In the *Single Briar Rose* (**Square 70**), the curved-line stroke is used twice, once for shading the petals and once to create dark, short curved lines as accents along the petal's edge. In *Wild Rose Corner* (**Square 71**), the long curved-line stroke is used to make the veining in the leaves. Here, the veining line curve is worked from the center of an area outward toward the element's edge.

Square 70

Square 71

Figure 2.32. Curved lines.

Sun Rays or Grass Strokes

This sample (see **Figure 2.33**) contains small half circles created from dashed lines that create the feeling of eyelashes, grass, or sun rays (**Square 41**). This would make an excellent texture to add a little interest to large open areas in a design. As an example, the sun rays worked on the practice board would make a wonderful wallpaper design behind a still life. The sun ray stroke, however, is most often used in landscape woodburning. This small pattern quickly adapts itself to become clusters of background trees (**Square 72**), clumps of leaves, and large sections of tall grass (**Square 73**).

Square 41

Square 72

Square 73

Figure 2.33. Sun rays and grass strokes.

Practice designs

Use your practice board to work small copies of the elements within a new design. Trace just a small section of your pattern into the squares on your board, just enough so that you can try that element before you work on your project. I have included small samples of some of the common design elements used for the patterns in this book.

Close-Up Tree Branches and Leaves

Figure 2.34 is a small section of tree branches from *The End of the Road* (**Square 58**). The branch areas were not burned; instead, these areas were surrounded with small dash strokes (**Squares 1–5**) to create clusters of leaves. When the leaves were finished, the branch showed as the original coloring of the wood. Notice the value changes in the leaf clumps; some are light, some are dark, and a few bottom clumps were burned to very dark tones.

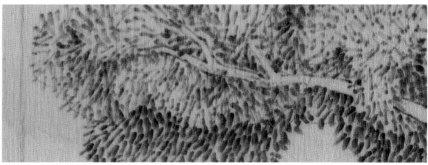

Figure 2.34. Thin clusters of leaves upheld on thin branches are often a mid-ground or foreground element. They can be used to fill the upper corners of a design, creating a framed look.

Square 58

Wood Grain Texture

This practice pattern (see **Figure 2.35**) is from *Hide 'n Seek* and is taken from an area in the wagon's side (**Square 59**). Wooden planks have fantastic textures and changing shapes. Note the half-circle knothole along the upper edge of the sample. There is a full knothole in the middle right and an area of wide grain in the lower middle left. This is the wavy-line texture pattern (Square 54) put to use to create the wood grain lines of the plank.

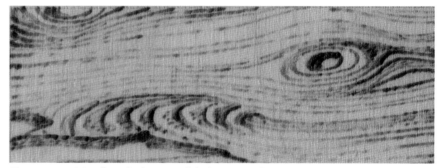

Figure 2.35. Wooden planks are a delight to woodburn because they can contain so many small details, such as grain lines, knot holes, and nails.

Square 59

Tall Grass and Grass Clumps

This grass element (see **Figure 2.36**), found in *The End of the Road*, *Our Town Mantel*, and *The Country Church*, is worked from the sun rays pattern and its variations (Squares 41, 72–73). It is a great foreground design that gives accent to the fine detailing in landscape patterns. Clumps of grass are darkest at the ground line, are medium toned in the middle section, and turn to pale tones as the individual blades of grass reach out from the central clump (**Square 60**). Small seed heads can be created by tapping the tool along a blade of grass.

Figure 2.36. Many landscapes use leaf clusters at the top of the design; the lower areas of the scene contain grass clumps. Grasses can include large, curved, sweeping leaves, small tree-branch-like structures, and grass heads. These clumps make a great frame finish for the bottom section of your scene.

Square 60

Small Crosshatched Elements

The flour bag in *Hide 'n Seek* (see **Figure 2.37**) was created by using a tightly packed crosshatch texture (**Squares 24–32**). By tracing this element to the practice board, I was able to work out the shaded areas that would make the flour bag three-dimensional in appearance (**Square 65**). Added layers of crosshatching were used to darken the inside part of the bag and the lower left side. Once the shading was completed, the wheat emblem and stitching were burned.

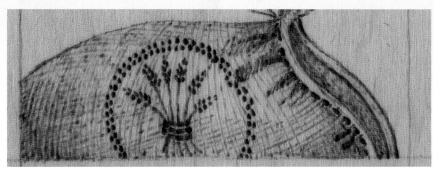

Square 65

Figure 2.37. When I have a pattern that contains some element that I have not burned before, such as this flour bag, I often do a small practice burn on my practice board or on a scrap of the same wood species that I am working.

Background Trees

As you work through *The Country Church* on page 155, you will create different types of background trees (see **Figure 2.38**). This is the test sample for those trees. The dark evergreens (**Square 75**) were done with a short dash stroke (**Squares 1–5**). It was easiest to turn the practice board upside down for this burning and to work the pines from the tree's tip toward its base.

The deciduous tree (**Square 76**) has very little detailing in the leaves. The branches were outline burns with a scrubby-line fill (**Squares 61–64**) for the tree trunk. Random, chaotic zigzagging (Square 40) creates the impression of new leaves.

  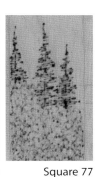

Square 75   Square 76   Square 77

Figure 2.38. Pines, evergreens, and deciduous trees are an important part of any landscape burning. These trees will be used in the background areas to frame off a building or along fencerows and roadsides.

Square 77 shows a cluster of pines and some small deciduous scrubs. These are far background elements, so the burning needed to be done in the pale tones to push the tree clump behind the main trees. Medium-toned dash strokes (Squares 1–5) make up the pines; the lower scrubs were burned using a random zigzag (Square 40).

Building Construction and Wall Construction

Figure 2.39 shows several parts of *The Country Church*. The left-hand sample (**Square 78**) shows the shadows created by the roof overhang, the board siding, and the zero value of the cross.

The middle section (**Squares 74** and **79**) shows the test samples for the stone walkway and for a board pattern that I could have used for the church siding. For both patterns, the surrounding areas rather than the element were burned. Only small details are needed on the elements themselves.

The right-hand sample (**Squares 81** and **80**) shows a small pine and scrub that was used as a middle ground element in *The Country Church*. Notice how this pattern has more definition and a deeper tonal value than the background clump of pines and scrubs.

Square 74   Square 81

Square 78   Square 79   Square 80

Figure 2.39. Many different textures can be burned to create the walls and roofs of buildings in a landscape. By practicing several different patterns, you can easily change a board and batten church into a stonewalled barn.

The church walls could have been stone, brick, or wood, so I did a test sample of each. This way, I could practice and then choose which one I wanted to use.

Patterns for Practice

Now that you've worked on how to create light and dark areas and textures and you've worked on a practice board, I wanted to give you some patterns for trying some of the different techniques. Go ahead and try the whole pattern if you want, or you can just try parts of the pattern to further explore its listed skill. Unless otherwise stated, the practice projects in this chapter were worked using the variable-temperature tool with the writing tip on birch plywood. If you are working with the one-temperature tool, please use the universal tip. Heat settings are noted for each project.

Light and Dark Exercise One: Temperature of the Tip

The wheat design used in *Our Daily Bread*, pattern on page 106, is created with a simple straight-line fill texture (see **Figure 2.40** and **Squares 66–68** on page 41). The coloring of each line in the wheat—whether it is light, medium, or dark—is controlled by the temperature of the tool. Notice in this finished sample that all of the woodburned lines run vertically within the design and that no element of the pattern has been outlined.

Figure 2.40. *Our Daily Bread.* Even though this burning uses only one texture, the straight line, it has three distinct tonal values: dark, medium, and light. How cool or hot you set your variable-temperature tool determines the tonal value of the burned stroke.

Tips for completing the entire pattern:

- Use a medium-high or high setting to burn the sections that are turned back on the bottom cross leaves and the tall pale leaves.

- The lettering is done in very close, tightly packed, short lines to create the darkest burning on the board.

1 Here is a small wheat pattern that you can use on your practice board to learn to control the tonal values through your temperature settings on your variable-temperature tool.

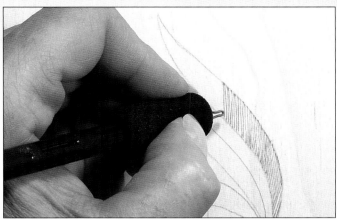

2 Once the sample pattern has been traced (see page 24 for transferring techniques), set your thermostat to a very low setting. Start your project with the tallest pale leaf. Pull long, light-colored lines from the top of the leaf to the bottom section, touching the traced line at both points. Fill that leaf with closely packed parallel lines using your writing tip.

3 Turn your thermostat up to a medium temperature setting. Fill the second wheat leaf with parallel lines using the writing tip. Notice that these lines burn slightly darker than the lines in the first leaf.

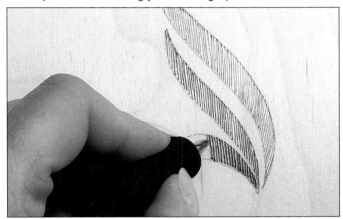

4 By turning up your thermostat one more time to a medium-high or high setting, you can now fill the last, third leaf with dark-toned lines.

5 The wheat head has three rows of seeds. The center row is burned using a low setting; the right side row uses a medium setting; and the left side row, the stem, and the wheat whiskers are burned at a medium-high or high setting.

6 Once all of the burning is done, use a white artist's eraser to remove any remaining pencil graphite from the tracing and very lightly sand the surface with an emery board. Because each area was created using the same texture—the straight-line fill—the pattern's depth of color was established solely through the temperature settings of the tool.

Light and Dark Exercise Two: Burning Time

For the pattern *Wild Rose Corner*, on page 111, the thermostat for the woodburning tool was set at a medium range throughout the work (see **Figure 2.41**). The changes in the coloring—the darkness of the wide borderline to the lightness of the leaves—were determined by how long the tool remained on the wood during the burning. Slow strokes create the dark areas; faster strokes make light lines.

Tips for completing the entire pattern:

■ Begin by working the texture pattern that lies behind the borderlines and flower design. This texture is a simple swirl design, created by moving your tool in very small, random curls (see **Squares 33–37** on page 41) across the wood. Start this curl pattern at the inner corner of the wide borderline; this is your darkest area for the background work. Move the tool slowly throughout this area to burn a medium-toned coloring. As you work away from the corner toward the outside of the pattern area, increase the speed with which you move your tool. Slightly faster burning will create paler curled lines. Continue filling in the background, gradually increasing the speed of your stroke until you can barely see the burn lines along the farthest edges of the work.

■ The stems on the rose are done with short straight-line fill strokes (see Squares 66–68 on page 41), allowing the tool to touch the wood long enough to create a medium-dark tone. The dark shading in the rose stems is done by repeating the burning over these areas. This gives two layers to the shaded side of the stem.

■ The outline on the flower petals is darker at the base of the flower and becomes pale toward the outer edge.

■ The veins in the flower petals, rosebud, flower center, and leaves are done in gently curved lines (see Squares 69–70 on page 41) at a medium stroke speed.

■ Work the petal lines from both the outer edge of the petal toward the center and then from the center of the flower toward the center creating two sets of lines within each petal.

■ Work the flower center from the central circle.

■ Use tightly packed spots (see Square 56 on page 41) to create small dots on the center lines of the rose and in the deep areas of the rosebud.

Figure 2.41. *Wild Rose Corner.* A wide range of values can be created just by learning to control how much time you use to make an individual burned stroke.

1 This three rose leaf pattern will let you learn how the speed of the tool affects the tonal value of the burned line or area. As with the exercise for *Our Daily Bread*, this small design can be worked on your practice board.

2 Trace the design to your practice board. Set the temperature of your variable-temperature tool to a medium heat. Start by outlining the leaves. Move the tool slowly so that the tool tip can burn a dark line along the edge of each leaf. Increase your speed as you approach a stop area. Notice where the leaf notches touch. The line closest to that joint is darker than the line at the tip of the leaf.

3 Begin the stroke at the center vein and pull your tool toward the outer edge of the leaf. The veins are done in gently curved lines (see Squares 69–70 on page 41) at a medium stroke speed. Notice how the line is darkest where it touches the center vein and then pales as you pull the tool away from that vein. This happens because your tool tip is hottest when it first touches the wood. As the tip is pulled through a stroke it begins to cool slightly, therefore lightening the end of the burned line. You can use this to your advantage in a design. Starting the stroke, its darkest point, at the center vein area of a leaf, for example, gives emphasis to the center vein.

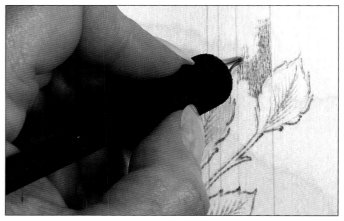

4 The large wide line behind the leaves is worked with a scrubby line texture and even, smooth movement.

5 Watch the color of the burning as you begin working this area. If the color seems pale, slow the tip movement to allow more burning time with each stroke. An early dark tone may mean that you need to move the tool more quickly to achieve a medium tonal value.

6 The thin background line is filled with a tightly packed spot that is created by touching the tool tip to the board then lifting. This touch-and-lift action creates small dark dots on your board (see Square 56 on page 41).

7 To develop a small amount of contrast color, or tone, in the background behind the white, unburned areas of the leaves, a curled line or circular stroke is used with a quick, flowing motion. Faster movements with your tool tips burn very pale shades of brown. I found it easier to turn the board upside down for this step.

8 When the burning is complete, erase any remaining pencil tracing lines and lightly sand. Although the heat setting was never changed during this exercise, you can create a wide variety of brown tones with just the speed of the movement of your burning tip.

Light and Dark Exercise Three: Layers of Strokes

The light and dark areas in the design *Ivy Line*, pattern on page 110, were created by adding layer upon layer of burned strokes to the areas (see **Figure 2.42**). The number of layers determines the lightness or darkness of each element within the pattern. The simplest stroke for layer work is the tightly spaced crosshatch pattern (see Squares 24–32 on page 41). Here, straight lines are laid down with all of the lines in that layer going in one direction. With each new layer the lines are burned in a new direction. I used a medium heat setting for this exercise.

Tips for completing the entire pattern:

- *Ivy Line* has four different shades of light and dark: There is a very pale set of leaves that uses one layer of lines (1), the medium-colored leaves use two layers (2), the darkest leaves use three layers (3), and the borderline is done in a short-line fill texture (4). This design is not outlined.

- The borderlines are burned using tightly packed spots (see Square 56 on page 41).

Figure 2.42. *Ivy Line.* How many layers of texturing you choose to burn determines how dark an area will become. Layering can easily take an area from very pale linen tones to the darkest tones of black.

1 A simple ivy leaf pattern is perfect for learning to use layers of burning to create tonal value changes in a project. Add this small design to your practice board.

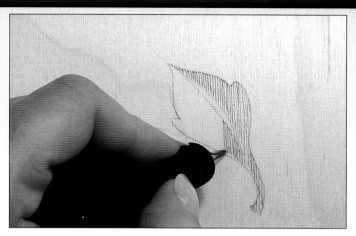

2 Begin burning tightly packed parallel lines into both sides of the leaf pattern at a 45-degree angle to the design (see Square 24 on page 41). Space your lines evenly as you work. Notice in the sample that the width of the unburned wood is about the same size as the width of the burned line. Start each line at the top of the pencil tracing line and pull it until it touches the bottom tracing line of that section of leaf.

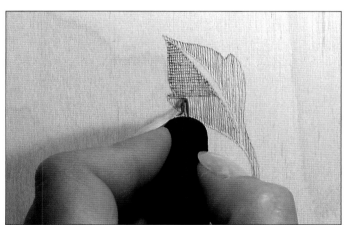

3 On one side of the leaf, burn a second layer of tightly packed parallel lines. These lines should run 90 degrees to the lines in your first layer of burning (see Square 25 on page 41). Notice that this second layer makes that side of the leaf darker in tone then the other side.

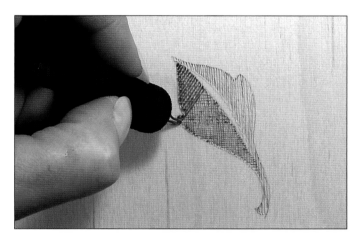

4 A third layer of tightly packed parallel lines has been burned into the dark side of the leaf. This layer is worked at a 45-degree angle to the previous layer (see Square 26 on page 41). You should have two very different colors, or tones, of brown in the two sides of your leaf when you are done with the third layer.

5 When the work is complete, erase your pencil lines and lightly sand. Changing the number of layers you burn with crosshatching is a simple and foolproof way to create different tonal values.

Light and Dark Exercise Four: Texture Pattern

So far in our practice projects we have used straight lines, crosshatching, random curls, and the short-line fill stroke, but any pattern of burning can be used to create the dark and light areas in your woodburning design (see **Figure 2.43**). For *My Room Gingerbread Man*, pattern on page 112, I chose to burn the background areas using three capital letters: A, B, and C (see Square 46 on page 41). Be creative with the texture pattern that you choose for this project. This pattern could easily be done by using 1, 2, 3 or by using a child's name, such as "AMY" or "JEFFREY." The words "My Room" could also be replaced with your child's name. I used a medium setting for this exercise.

The *My Room Gingerbread Man* pattern is too detailed to practice just a part, so we will practice the negative space technique with the letter *A*. In order to form a negative element, shading must be especially dark on the borders of the object to emphasize and define its edges. I chose random curls for this exercise, but you can choose any fun texture you want!

Tips for completing the entire pattern:

- Although I have burned my sample on a piece of birch plywood, this particular pattern would be delightful done on a gingerbread man cut-out shape or a door hanger sign.

- Using a T-square, ruler, and soft #4B to #6B pencil, mark guidelines across the wood for your letter placement. Since this pattern is about 12" tall, I used a spacing of ⅛".

- When you reach an area on the inner design—the eyes, mouth, icing trim, or words "My Room"—stop burning. Notice with this pattern that the woodburned areas are used to surround the actual important elements of the design.

Figure 2.43. *My Room Gingerbread Man.* Not only has this design been worked with an unusual texturing pattern, it is also done as a negative pattern, or negative image. The woodburning has been worked to surround the main elements (the lettering and face) of the pattern and therefore make the unburned areas of the gingerbread man stand out.

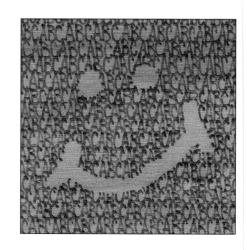

1 Add this small pattern to your practice board.

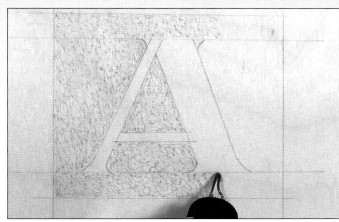

2 Working with any of the three techniques that we are discussing in this section—temperature, burning time, and layers—begin to shade in all of the space surrounding the letter A to a pale or light tone of brown.

3 As you work, darken the areas that are nearest the letter *A* to a medium tone. Notice how the letter begins to stand out from its background even though you have done no woodburning to the letter itself.

4 Your darkest tonal value of brown should be where the background directly touches the letter. Don't outline the letter; instead, darken the background.

5 Erase your guidelines and pattern lines, and then lightly sand the surface. Dark tonal values can make unburned or unworked areas of your project stand out against their brown backgrounds. Dramatic changes in tonal values create a striking finish for a pattern.

Light and Dark Exercise Five: Putting It All Together

In *Buffalo Skull Dream Weaver Circle*, pattern on page 134, I have put all of these methods together to create a work that has several points of interest (see **Figure 2.44**). The first thing that you may notice is the dramatic changes in shading. The paleness of the buffalo skull is balanced by the extremely dark surrounding circles of the dream catcher. Second, each area of the woodburning has its own texturing stroke. Because this exercise includes so many different textures and techniques, we will be working with the whole pattern instead of using a portion of the pattern as we did with the previous exercises.

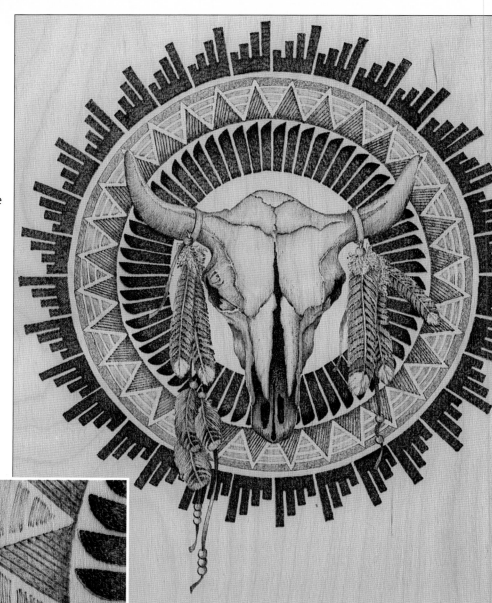

Figure 2.44. *Buffalo Skull Dream Weaver Circle.* Most woodburning patterns use temperature, time, texture, and layering to create distinct tonal values. The *Buffalo Skull Dream Weaver Circle* is an excellent pattern to practice and experiment with the four ingredients.

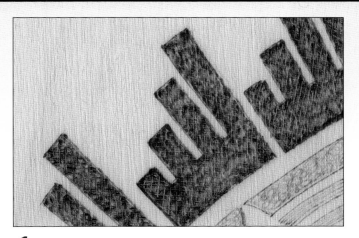

1 The outer ring was created by using tightly packed, straight, diagonal lines; a medium-high temperature; and a slow rate of movement. Several layers of this stroke were burned until the area had a dark, even coloring.

2 The next ring is made of short straight-line fill strokes (see Square 66 on page 41) on a medium temperature and with a medium time for burning, while the inner sections of this pie-shaped wedge are straight lines. The inner pie wedges were first darkly burned with widely spaced, straight, diagonal lines (see Square 15 on page 41). Then, layers of random curls (see Squares 33–37 on page 41) were applied over the lines. Once a medium-dark tone was achieved, one more layering of random curls was added along the inner edge of the circle to deepen this line.

3 The last ring is made up of feather-shaped curved-line strokes (see Squares 69–70 on page 41). These were burned at a high temperature setting and with a small dash stroke pattern (see Squares 1–5 on page 41) by letting the tool tip rest for a moment to create the dark tone. Along the outer edge of this feather shape, a second layer of dash stroke pattern was added to darken the tips to a black coloring.

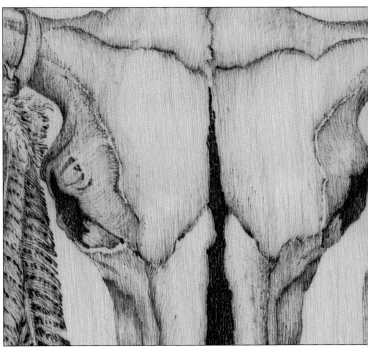

4 The buffalo skull design was burned using a fine-line texturing at low temperatures. This work is very similar to the work in *Our Daily Bread*. Layer upon layer of fine lines were added to darken the shadows of each area, giving the skull a three-dimensional finish. The black areas within the skull are filled with the small-dot pattern at a high temperature until these areas are as black as the inner circle feather shapes.

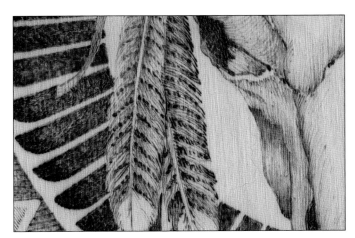

5 The feathers that hang from the buffalo's horns are done in short curved-line strokes (see Square 70 on page 41). A central line to the feathers was first burned, and then finer lines were added, working from that centerline out toward the edge of the feather.

Texture Exercise One: Putting Textures Together

Figure 2.45. This design, *Solar Flare Sun Face*, uses eight distinct textures: crosshatching, dash strokes, wavy lines, random curls, seashell circles, herringbone, diagonal lines, and detail outlining. This was all worked on heartwood birch plywood, which adds more texture to the finished design because of the changing grain pattern in the wood.

This *Solar Flare Sun Face,* pattern on page 141, is a fun pattern to try if you want to explore the multiple textures that you can use in woodburning (see **Figure 2.45**). To add to the fun look of *Solar Flare Sun Face*, I chose a very grain-sculptured piece of heartwood birch plywood for the project. Not only is the sun face full of changing patterns and textures, but so is the unburned background because of its dramatic graining. Try this design using the texture patterns that most interest you from the practice board, as well as experimental texture patterns of your own! Here again, we will be working with the whole pattern instead of using a portion of the pattern as we did with the previous exercises. I used a medium heat setting throughout this exercise.

1 For my sample, I used tight-spaced crosshatching (see Squares 24–32 on page 41) to establish the shadows and shading in the face. Adding more layers of crosshatching created the darker facial shadings.

2 Touching the tool tip to the wood to burn tightly packed, small dots (see Square 56 on page 41) gave the eyes, nostrils, and mouth the black-chocolate coloring.

3 The wavy-line texture (see Square 42 on page 41) was used to create the sun face's mustache. Over this texturing, a light layering of random curls (see Squares 33–37 on page 41) made the mustache darker where it touched the bottom of the nose.

4 The diamond shapes that surround the sun face were filled with the seashell circle texture (see Square 43 on page 41).

5 The sun flare leaves have a herringbone straight-line burn (see Square 53 on page 41) worked from the centerline out toward the flare's edge. Detail lines were first burned into the curling flares that make up the hair. Over this detailing, random curls (see Squares 33–37 on page 41) were laid to create the shading. New layers of random curls were burned to darken these flares where one flare tucked under another. The stars were filled in with two layers of diagonal lines.

6 Once all of the texturing and shading were completed, I added the outline burn to each element.

Composition of a Good Woodburning

Now that we have taken a look at how to create the various tones and textures with your woodburning tool, we want to take a look at how all of the elements interact to create a complete picture. Understanding tonal values, or the different shades of color that we've been discussing, is one of the keys to creating a pleasing finished project. These values can be used to give one element or area of a woodburning more emphasis than the rest of the design. They can also help you translate real images into a woodburning project.

In addition to tonal values, we'll explore a variety of techniques, including how to make the most of your unburned areas, effective ways to outline your projects, and how to use textures in conjunction with each other. By taking the time to learn both the techniques for creating shades and textures and the concepts for putting them all together, you'll be able to confidently woodburn a cohesive finished piece.

Understanding tonal values

If you have been working through the book from the beginning, you are already a little familiar with the concept of tonal values. Any time we have been working with shades of color, we have been working with tonal values. Understanding tonal value, also called gray scale, and its use in a woodburning pattern will greatly enhance the quality of your work.

What Exactly Are Tonal Values?

The human eye gathers information about an object or a scene in two separate ways: the amount of light that strikes an object and the color of the object. Once the eye has determined both the light value and color value of an object, the information is merged to create the image that we see. So, although we see a shiny red apple that casts a shadow, the eye first sees the shine and the shadow, then sees the red, and finally creates the total image of a three-dimensional, highlighted red object with a shadow.

Highlights and shadows are called tonal values and range from the darkest black to the brightest white area of an image. Shades of brown and gray are also considered tonal values. Colors, called hues, include the primary hues of red, yellow, and blue. You can mix hues and tonal values. As an example, pastel yellow is a mixture of the primary hue of yellow and the white tonal value. Navy blue is a mixture of the primary color blue and the tonal value of black.

Pyrography works in the same manner. First, we create the woodburning using tonal values from very dark brown through the palest tones of our wood surface. Once the burning is completed, coloring can be placed over top of the burned surface. This merges the two areas of information exactly as the human eye does.

Finding the Tonal Values in a Photo or Drawing

Whether you are working from a pencil drawing, a black-and-white photograph, or a burned sample from this book to create your woodburning, you will first want to number the tonal values from the darkest area of the image to the brightest white area. Exploring the finished burning of *The Philadelphia Derringer*, you will note that the woodburning is created in only one color (see **Figure 2.46**). Every part of the design is brown. This is called a monochromatic image, mono meaning "one" and chromatic meaning "color." So, it is a one-color design. What creates the picture is the brown used in various tonal values. The work has areas that range from no burning at all to very pale browns to a black-brown value.

By numbering the values first, you can discover where your blackest and whitest points in the burning will be, discover areas of similar value for easy burning, and identify each area before you begin. Throughout this chapter, I'll show you how to identify and number each of the different values in a photo.

As you are doing the value numbering of a photo or drawing, you will want to watch for areas that might cause you problems during the composition stage or woodburning process. This particular still life is set up in a triangular composition with the elements—the derringer, the books, and the pipes—all contained within the left and bottom section of the photo. The upper section and right side contain no elements. So, the bottom left of the photo is full, but the upper right half is empty. I wanted to work *The*

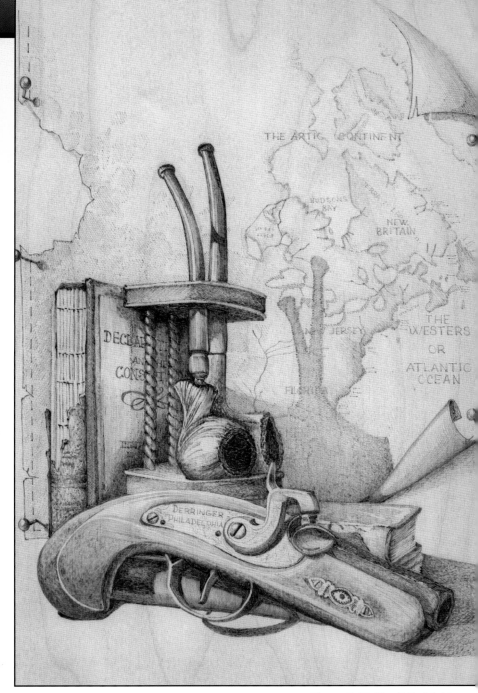

Philadelphia Derringer* on a rectangular board, so I added an old map, pinned to the wall, as a background element. This fills the empty area behind the still life. Since this map design was added after the photo and after the value numbering process, it is not shown in the photos. However, because the map will hang on the wall behind the still life, I worked the map in the same tonal value as the wall in the photo.

Figure 2.46. *The Philadelphia Derringer* is a good example of a tonal value woodburning. Note that the darkest areas of the burning are found in the shadows under the derringer, inside the briar pipes, and under the roof of the pipe rack. The palest, or lightest, values are used for the book pages, background map, and gunmetal.

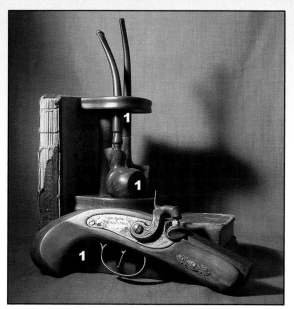

Figure 2.47. The darkest areas of the photo are numbered. These shadows form the black, or darkest, value: Value #1.

Value #1—Black (darkest value)

To establish the tonal values of a woodburned picture, begin with either a pencil drawing of your design or a photograph. If you have access to a computer and scanner, scan the photo into the computer. Using a graphics program, change that photo to grayscale. This removes all of the color information from the photo, leaving only the shadows and highlights. Most digital cameras on the market today have editing programs that can be used to make grayscale images. Two of the many excellent graphics programs available to an artist are Paint Shop Pro and Adobe Photoshop. Please refer to the Help section of your computer program for use and instructions.

I find it easiest to establish the tonal values of a still life by working from the darkest to the lightest areas. First, find the very black shadows of the photo and mark these as Value #1.

For the photo of the Derringer still life, the darkest areas (see **Figure 2.47**) are the inside of the front briar pipe, the shadow cast by the derringer onto the books, and the area underneath the top section of the pipe rack. The smaller areas of black have not been numbered. They are the right edge of the standing book's binding, the area where the standing book's side meets the backdrop, the inside of the gun's barrel, and the shadow on the back pipe's stem.

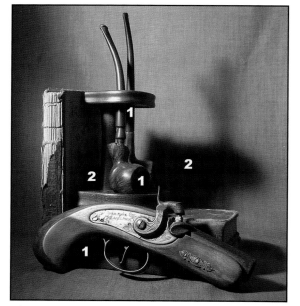

Figure 2.48. Value #2 comprises areas that are just a bit lighter than the black values of Value #1.

Value #2—Dark chocolate (dark value)

Next, look for black tones that are not quite as dark as those already noted. These are Value #2.

The photo shows Value #2 (see **Figure 2.48**) on the lower portion of the right side of the standing book and in the large shadow on the backdrop. The left side of the backdrop in the photo would also be a Value #2; however, since our still life design will have an antique map as its background, this area in the photo will not become part of the finished burning. The added map will use the Value #2 setting of the backdrop.

Value #3—Milk chocolate (medium-dark value) Still working with the dark values of the photo, these areas that are just a touch paler than the last are marked as Value #3 (see **Figure 2.49**). Notice that with each numbering you are looking for areas that are slightly lighter in value than the last.

The Value #3 areas are the upper portion of the standing book's right side, the front binding of the standing book, and the shadows under the trigger guard and to the right of the book stack.

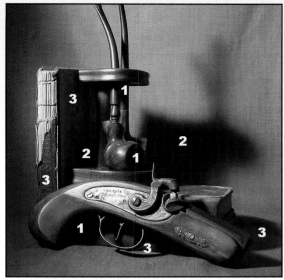

Figure 2.49. Milk chocolate tones make up the areas of Value #3.

Value #4—Coffee with cream (medium value)
You know that soft, milky mocha look that coffee with cream has? That's the tonal value that you now want to mark (see **Figure 2.50**). It is the middle tonal value in this photo, or Value #4.

The middle values, Value #4, are located on the gunstock and the top cover of the book stack. The edges of the stacked books and the gun's hammer mechanism are also Value #4 but are too small to mark in the photo.

Figure 2.50. Label the milky mocha colors as the medium values for Value #4.

Value #5—Tanned leather (light-medium value)
Those areas that are lighter than the medium tones are next numbered as Value #5 (see **Figure 2.51**).

Value #5 tones are the backdrop cloth sections to the right side of the book stack, below the derringer, and above the standing book. An antique map will appear in the pattern in these areas.

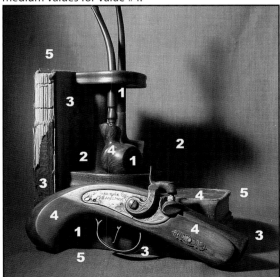

Figure 2.51. Tanned leather colors make up the light-medium values of Value #5.

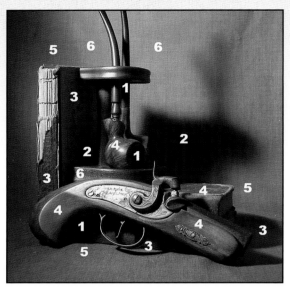

Figure 2.52. Light values in the photo, colored like caramel candy, are marked as Value #6.

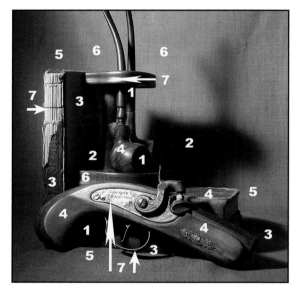

Figure 2.53. The lightest values of the work, similar to a pale linen color, are noted as Value #7.

Figure 2.54. The unburned portions of the design are Value #0.

Value #6—Caramel (light value)

The pale tones of a woodburning often take on the coloring of a caramel candy and are noted as Value #6 (see **Figure 2.52**).

For our sample, these pale shadings are found to the left and right of the pipe stems and in the base of the pipe rack. The two marked areas surrounding the pipe stems will be burned into the antique map background of the pattern.

Value #7—Linen (palest value)

The palest values in a woodburning still have color in them. They are likened to a pale linen and become Value #7 (see **Figure 2.53**).

The lightest shades of tonal value in this photo are found in the damaged area of the standing book's binding and as highlights in the pipe rack. The tipper guard edge and metal plate on the side of the derringer are also extremely pale. These areas are numbered as Value #7.

Value #0—Unburned areas

There will be areas of any pattern that you do not woodburn. The original coloring of the wood, therefore, becomes the whitest areas of the work. These areas can be noted as Value #0, the zero representing the lack of burning. If I had not included the map in the final burning, all of the area in the background of the still life, except the cast shadows, would have been marked as Value #0 (see **Figure 2.54**).

In this design, the metal plate beneath the pistol's hammer, the highlights on the briar pipe, and the highlight along the pipe stem have all been left unburned wood, so they are Value #0 areas.

Transferring the Values

Once the tonal values have been established, you can transfer those value numbers to your pattern for quick reference as you work (see **Figure 2.55**). As a general rule of thumb, the larger the number of values that can be established in a design, the more realistic the finished burning will be. Photo-realistic woodburnings often begin with seven to nine distinct tonal values (see **Figure 2.56**). More simplistic burnings may have three to five tonal values.

As a beginning woodburner, keep the number of tonal values to a minimum, between three and five. This keeps the number of different tonal values small as you learn to burn light, medium, and dark areas into your work. As you grow in this craft, you will discover that you are adding more and more levels of tonal value.

In the top row of squares in Figure 2.56, I have cut samples of each of the tonal values used in this burning and placed them in order from darkest to lightest so that you can see the

progression of the tones. This row begins with a solid square of black color and ends with a solid square of beige that matches the birch wood that you can use as comparison to the burned values. The bottom row of squares is created to show some of the detailing and texturing used in *The Philadelphia Derringer.*

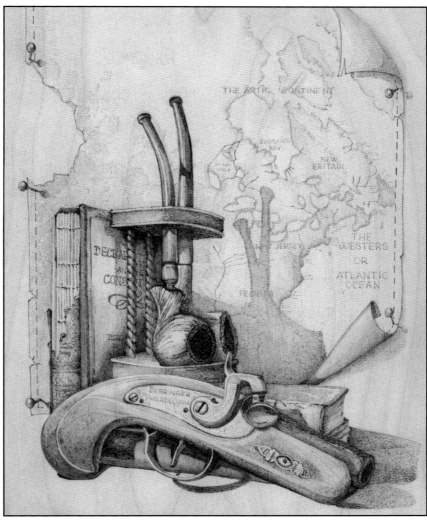

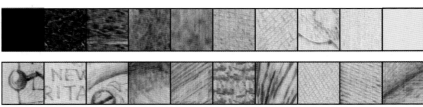

Figure 2.56. You can see the value scale below the derringer burning that shows the wide variety of sepia tones you can achieve in woodburning. A black square has been added to provide a comparison to the very darkest tones; the unburned square of birch is equal to the whitest value. Below the tonal values you can see some of the different textures and strokes used in this burning to create those tonal values.

Figure 2.55. By marking the value numbers on the traced pattern, you can create a map for the placement of your pale, medium, and dark tonal values.

Focusing attention

Tonal values can also be used to give one element or area of a woodburning more emphasis than the rest of the design. Areas of sharp tonal value contrast attract the eye whereas areas that are close in tonal value do not. By adding sharp contrast—like white values directly touching the blackest values—you pull the eye to that area of your work. If instead you burn an area with very similar values, whether they are all dark values or all pale values, that area becomes less noticeable.

In a landscape that contains a background, middle ground, and foreground, those elements that are contained in the background will be very similar in pale value. There will be little or no color difference between your mountains, sky, and distant tree lines. As you move forward in the landscape to the middle ground, the barns, roads, and fields in this area will move into the medium tonal values. These medium values will encompass a wider range of values, from beige through light brown, than the limited range of the pale background tones. It is not until you reach the foreground that you find distinct shades of black and white within the elements and definite shadows cast by those elements. The foreground of a woodburned landscape will contain areas of all of the tonal values from your palest white through to your blackest area of work. The foreground, therefore, has the widest range of tonal values in the work.

Very dark and black values have more impact than pale values. In any woodburning, your eye will find the blackest area of the work first. Making the most important element of the pattern also the darkest will force that element to stand out from its surrounding area.

The Harrisburg Star Barn shows how you can focus the attention of your woodburning scene by controlling the use of your tonal values (see **Figure 2.57**). Notice in this work how your eye goes directly to the barn; yet the areas behind the barn, the cloud bank, the areas in front of the barn, and the pond with the barn's reflection are just as detailed as the main barn. This happens because all of the burning in both the cloud bank and the pond reflection are very close in tonal values, so these areas become muted. There is no sharp contrast between light and dark in these areas.

The barn, however, has a very clear, distinct contrast between the white walls of the barn and the dark shadows of the open stall doors, barn overhang, and roof detailing. The eye naturally is attracted to areas of sharp contrast.

By eliminating any sharp contrast in the clouds and the pond and by emphasizing the contrast in the barn, I have made the focus of this scene the barn structure. This technique—controlled use of your tonal values—is excellent for woodburnings that have a great deal of detailing.

Figure 2.57. *Harrisburg Star Barn*. You can focus attention to one area of your design by using sharp contrasts between the light and dark tones in that area. The top row of squares shows samples cut from the burning of the tonal values that were used to create this work. You can see the progression from darkest to lightest value. The Star Barn's value range is compact with the changes between tonal values kept minimal. The bottom row shows texture samples and detailing from the burning.

Figure 2.58. *The End of the Road.* Textured patterns can be used to establish the tonal values of light through dark. Textures also add interest because of their changing patterns. The value changes, top row, are more dramatic than those in the *Harrisburg Star Barn*. The darkest tone used is very close to true black. This design incorporated a wide variety of textures to create the tonal values, bottom row.

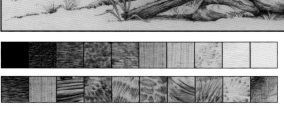

Adding texture

Texturing adds to a woodburning by creating repeating patterns of interest throughout the work. *The End of the Road* uses a wide variety of texture patterns to establish different elements in the scene (see **Figure 2.58**). Leaf patterns are repeated in both the foreground tree and the smaller background tree, while the pine needles of the spruce take on a new texture. When adding textured patterns to your work, continue those patterns within an element whether the tonal value is dark or light. Note on the foreground tree that the leaf texturing is done in both very pale tonal values and very dark ones. By varying the tonal values of those texture patterns, you can pull some of the leaf clumps forward with pale tones, tuck some of them into the middle section of the tree with medium values, and push some to the back into the shadows of the tree with darkly burned values.

Creating shadows

Shadows are created when light comes into contact with a solid element in the design. Since the light cannot pass through the object, there is an area of darkness on the opposite side of the element from the light source.

The tonal value of a shadow is determined by where it falls within the still life or landscape. Middle ground elements, for example, cast medium-valued shadows as compared to foreground elements, which cast very dark shadows. You can create an impression of depth to still lifes and landscapes by including shadowing. Adding a shadow area, especially in the foreground of a design, can eliminate the need to burn the ground, grass, or floor area of your design. Since a shadow must lie on the ground or floor, the shadow implies the ground area.

In *Hide 'n Seek* (see **Figure 2.59**), there is no woodburning where the ground should be. Instead, the ground line has been established by using only the shadow cast by the wagon.

This particular shadow contains a range of tonal values. Where the shadow is closest to the light source—between the front wheels—that shadow is a mid-tone value; but, where the shadow disappears under the wagon, it becomes the darkest value in the work. Using shadows can eliminate the need to detail or outline each and every object in the original drawing.

Figure 2.59. *Hide 'n Seek.* The shadow under the wagon gives the impression of ground without needing the details of rocks, grass, etc. Since shadows must always lie against a solid object, using a shadow in this way will give your project a background without too much effort. The range of tonal values in this particular shadow also gives more richness to the woodburning.

Using multiple techniques

Grandpa's Pride and Joy uses tonal values, focuses attention, has different textures, and uses shadows (see **Figure 2.60**). It contains a wide variety of tonal values, from extremely black areas to large areas that are nearly the tonal value of the birch plywood. Texturing is used throughout the scene to establish different elements. The leaf texturing is repeated in each of the trees; the grass texturing is the same for the background grass as well as the foreground clumps. A heavy shadow under the front bumper of the old car is used to create the idea of foreground grass, and the light value in the upper tree leaves is allowed to fade away into the unburned wood, implying more leaves. Finally, this scene uses the idea of sharp contrast in the car and foreground tree versus muted contrast in the background barn scene, thus focusing the viewer's attention on the old, rusted car.

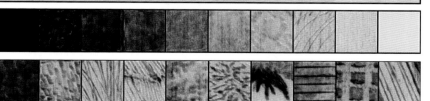

Outlining your design

Outlines are excellent for defining an area, especially when two touching elements are very close in tonal value or shading colors. They also give strength or importance to an area. For example, outlining some of the petals of a flower will bring your eye to those petals quicker than to those that are not outlined. Be cautious using an outline in your design. If you outline too much, the work will take on a coloring book look. Use just enough to accent the work and not overpower the design.

There are some designs that will use outlines along the edges of each element in the pattern. In general, the more stylized the design, the more outlining you will use. *Summer Morning Sun Face* is a very stylized pattern that can easily be adapted for a bold outline stroke (see **Figure 2.61**). Adding an outline stroke is best done after the shading and texturing have been completed and by using a medium temperature setting.

In this first sample of outlining, all of the traced pattern lines have been burned using a high temperature (see **Figure 2.62**). As you look at the outlines, you will see small spots of darker coloring in the lines (see **Figure 2.63**). These spots, or bubbles, are caused when the tool crosses from one grain line to another. Instead of a nice, straight, even line, you end up with a connect-the-dot appearance to the work. The more tightly packed the grain lines are in the wood surface, the more bubbles you will have in your outlining.

Here is the same pattern burned, but this time the outlining was done after the shading and texturing were completed (see **Figure 2.64**). There is still some bubbling along the outlines, but it has been

Figure 2.60. *Grandpa's Pride and Joy.* This burning uses texturing to create the different tonal values. The top row of squares shows how dramatic the tonal value changes are. The darkest value in nearly true black creates the strong contrast to the unburned birch wood. This pattern does not use a large variety of texture, bottom row; instead, the emphasis of the work is on tonal value contrast.

greatly reduced in size and number. This is because the earlier work of shading and texturing broke down the wood fibers, thus reducing the effects on the wood grain. Using a medium temperature for the outline strokes and burning several layers to the line give you greater control over your outlines.

Single Briar Rose has the appearance of outlining, yet very little line work was added after the pattern had been shaded and textured (see **Figure 2.65**). The outlines, or accent lines, that the pattern does have are along the left side of the stems and along the curved cutouts within each petal of the rose (see **Figure 2.66**). The feeling that each area has been outlined was created when the shading was applied. A woodburning stroke naturally begins with a darker tonal value at the start of the burn and a lighter tonal value toward the end of that stroke. Remember, this effect occurs because the tool is hottest when it touches the wood surface at the beginning of the stroke. As you pull the tool across the wood to complete the stroke, the tool tip begins to cool very slightly. This lightens the end of the burned stroke. By beginning each of the burning strokes along the pattern line—in this sample, I began them at the outer edge of the petals—I have used this dark-to-light tendency to my advantage.

Where you start a burning stroke determines where your darker shading for that line will be. On the leaves of *Single Briar Rose,* I began the burn strokes along the center vein of each leaf and pulled outward toward the leaf edge. Notice how this darkens the leaf centers, accenting the central leaf vein.

Figure 2.61. *Summer Morning Sun Face* is a stylized design easily adapted for a bold outline stroke.

Figure 2.62. All of the traced pattern lines have been burned using a high temperature.

Figure 2.63. When adding an outline stroke, be sure to complete the texturing and shading first. If you do not, the unsmoothed wood grain will cause small spots of darker coloring when the line crosses from one grain line to another.

Figure 2.64. Here the outlining was done after the shading and texturing were completed. This method greatly reduced the spots.

There are times when I will outline a more realistic pattern at the beginning of the woodburning process. If the pattern is extremely detailed and I will be working on it over an extended period of time, I will outline the general element lines of the design before any other work is done. So if my design is a barn landscape, I will outline the barn walls and roof but not every individual barn wall board or roof shingle. This general outlining is done is a very pale tonal value using a low setting on my thermostat. If during the working process some of my pencil tracing lines become smudged or need erasing, I still have the general outline set to use as a reference guide. Because some projects get set aside for a time period before you are able to complete the burning, this general pale outline ensures that your pattern lines will still be there when you get back to work. By working this outline in a very pale value, I can do darker value shading and accenting right over the outline work. As I work the tonal values of the rest of the design, the pale outline often disappears into the finished woodburning.

Figure 2.65. *Single Briar Rose* has the appearance of being outlined even though it does not actually have burned lines for each of the tracing lines.

Figure 2.66. The outlines, or accent lines, that the pattern does have are along the left side of the stems and along the curved cutouts within each petal of the rose.

Not every element must be burned

Just because a pattern includes line detail, it is not necessary to burn every single line or element within the design. Woodburning is a wonderful medium for fine details; however, an image can quickly become overpowered when there is too much for the eye to see. Leaving some areas unburned, and therefore open to the imagination of the viewer, adds to the composition of the work. Unburned or unworked parts within a design give the viewer contrasting areas to compare to highly detailed elements.

In this burned portrait, *Western Horse*, there is a large amount of detail work in the braided bridle and in the shadowing around the forehead, eye area, neck, cheek, and lower jaw (see **Figure 2.67**). These areas fall into a medium-dark tonal range. To balance this darkness, the top of the nose down to the mouth area, the forelock, and the ears have very little detailing, thus keeping these areas light in tonal value. By keeping the detailing in the light areas to a minimum, the face of the horse has an equal amount of lights and darks.

When the pattern was traced to the plaque, the horse's eye needed to fall along the centerline of the wood. This pushed the neck and mane very close to the edge of the plaque. Had I detailed the mane area, it would have darkened this area, making the pattern visually out of balance. All of the dark areas would have fallen on the right half of the plaque and below the plaque's center point. The light areas would have all been above the center and to the left.

Only a few hairs of the mane were needed to establish the boundaries of this area. Leaving the rest of the mane with little or no detailing kept the finished work nicely balanced from the center of the wood.

Grandpa's Pride and Joy also has a large area of the pattern unburned (see **Figure 2.68**). To make the old, rusted car the focal point of the work, I burned it to medium-dark tones. The areas under

the fender, under the bumper, and along the lower door edge are the darkest points of the piece and are layered to a deep shade of chocolate-black.

To contrast these black areas in the car, I wanted the foreground grass as pale as possible. So the only areas in the foreground that I burned were the watering can, fence posts, and front tree. The grass areas in front of the car's bumper and front wheel were not woodburned, allowing these areas to remain the original color of the wood. The black edge under the front bumper provided enough information to imply the foreground grass.

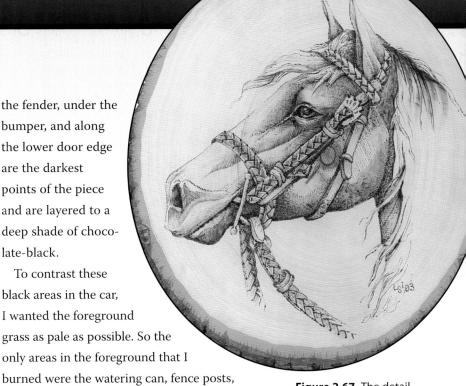

Figure 2.67. The detail work in the braided bridle and in the shadowing around the forehead, eye area, neck, cheek, and lower jaw fall into a medium-dark tonal range. To balance these darker areas, the top of the nose down to the mouth, the forelock, and the ears have very little detailing.

Figure 2.68. *Grandpa's Pride and Joy* also has a large area of unburned wood. The car was burned in medium-dark tones to make it the focal point of the work. The foreground section was left mostly unburned to provide contrast for the car.

Protecting Areas from Woodburning

When it is important to keep areas from being woodburned, low-tack masking tape and drafting tape can be used to protect areas from low-temperature burnings (see **Figure 2.69**). In this sample, *The Country Church*, the areas surrounding the roof of the church have been masked to create a strong, crisp edge. The shading for the roof can now be added, allowing the tool tip to cross over the roof area onto the tape. When the burning is complete, the tape can be removed and the wood underneath the tape will be unburned. This is a good technique when you want to use a random texture, such as curls, for shading yet still desire a straight edge to the area being worked.

Be careful when using masking tape as a protective layer because it can lift small wood fibers where it is applied. It is advisable to first test the tape on a small corner of your project or on the back of the wood surface. Masking tape can take medium temperatures of burning; however, high temperatures will soften the tape's adhesive. The adhesive will need to be removed from the wood surface with a white artist's eraser or be rubbed off with your finger before that area is worked. Again, test this masking tape technique on your wood surface before you use it on your project.

Shape versus coloring in a pattern

Each area or element of a design will have both shape and color. For example, the trees in an autumn landscape may be red, gold, and orange in color, but those same trees in a summer scene will be medium and dark green. However, the shape of the trees does not change because the season changes. So, the leaf clumps will still have a rounded feeling, and the tree branches will still go beneath, or into, the leaves. Knowing which parts of your design are shapes and which show color will help to create a more realistic woodburning.

The owl's feathers in *Horned Owl* come in a variety of shapes and positions all over this bird of prey (see **Figure 2.70**). Notice the fine half-circle feathers that make up the wing shoulder and compare them to the longer flight feathers lower on the wing. The feathers along the breast area and leggings are fine, fuzzy down. Each grouping, or clump, of feathers on this bird has a curved shape and casts shadows on other groupings of feathers depending on their position along the body.

The feathers of the horned owl also have a variety of coloring patterns. The long flight feathers and tail feathers have dark-colored bars; the breast feathers have speckling and a dark spotting color. Those feathers that create the eye ring end with a dark band at the outer edge.

Figure 2.69. Low-tack masking tape and drafting tape can be used to protect areas from low-temperature burnings.

Figure 2.70. Notice the different types of feathers that make up this image. Each group of feathers casts shadows on other groupings of feathers depending on their position along the body. Burn the shapes as a first step.

This can seem to be a large amount of information to try to capture in just one woodburning work. Dividing the image into working steps—one for shape, one for shadows, and the last one for color—makes the work much easier.

The image above shows the *Horned Owl* burned for the shape of each grouping of feathers and for the shadows those feather groups cast on other feathers (see Figure 2.70). Once the bird had a strong, three-dimensional form, the color bands and patterns were laid over top of the earlier work (see **Figure 2.71**).

Therefore, by first woodburning the shape of each feather group, then adding the shadows, and finally adding the color information, *Horned Owl* becomes a very realistic burning.

Figure 2.71. The feathers of the horned owl also have a variety of coloring patterns, made up of dark-colored bars, speckling, and dark spotting. Burn the shape of the body, the head, and the wings first; then, add the color area burnings as a second step.

Tonal Value Project: *The Pocket Watch*

Tip: Writing tip or universal tip

Wood: White birch plywood, 8" x 12"

Tonal values: Very dark, dark, medium, and light

Textures: Scrubby line (Squares 61–64), curved line (Squares 69–70), tightly packed spots (Square 56), wide crosshatch pattern (Squares 15–23), tight crosshatch pattern (Squares 24–32), outline

The Pocket Watch is perfect for learning more about tonal values. This design has been broken down into six steps: one for the outlining of the design, four steps focusing on one tonal value each, and one step for finishing.

The Pocket Watch measures 8" wide by 12" high. My sample was worked on birch plywood using a variable-temperature tool and a writing tip, but you can use a one-temperature tool also. The thermostat temperatures were changed throughout this burning. The textures used in this project are shown on the practice board (see page 41). Throughout this step-by-step project, I will be showing the settings that work for me with my variable-temperature tool. You will want to adjust those settings to fit your practice settings chart according to the wood that you have chosen to burn.

This will be a very quick project because the face of the clock, the largest pattern section, is not burned. It remains the original color of the wood. As you work, focus on establishing four individual color tones and keeping those color tones the same throughout the design.

Although the finished piece was worked as a picture, this would be a delightful design made as an actual wall clock (see the Creating a Real Wall Clock section on page 87).

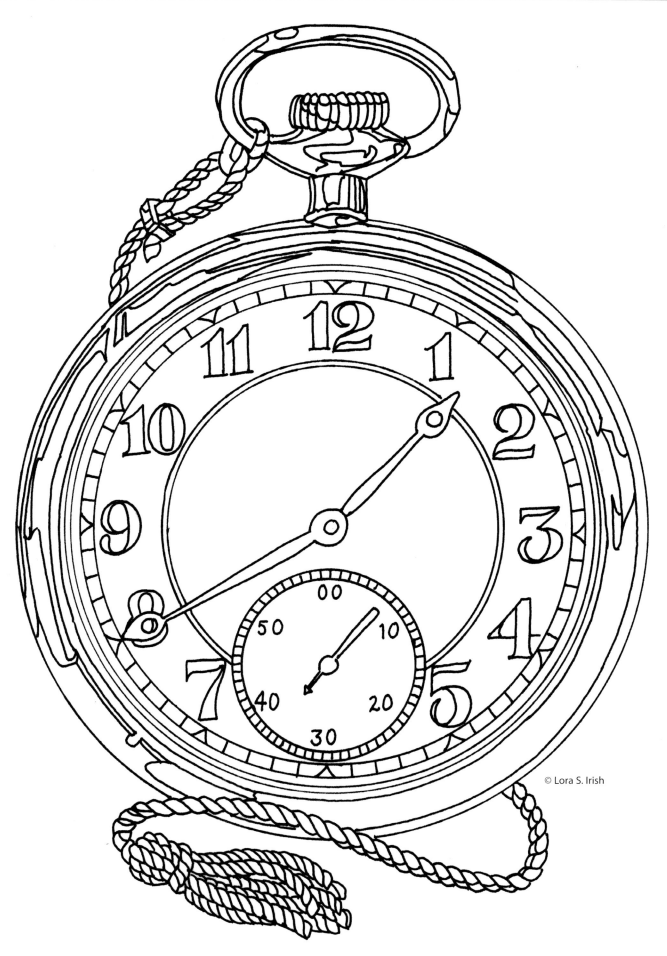

© Lora S. Irish

Step 1: Tracing and Outlining

Begin the work by lightly sanding your plywood with fine-grit sandpaper. Remove any sanding dust with a lint-free cloth or large drafter's dusting brush. Make a tracing of the pattern onto vellum or onionskin tracing paper. Rub the back of the tracing paper with a soft pencil until you have created a dark, even layer of graphite. Tape the pattern paper to your board and retrace the pattern lines. Trace only those lines that you need to guide you through the work. With a white artist's eraser, rub off any smudges or streaks left during the tracing process. Set your thermostat to a medium-high temperature. With the writing tip, outline all of the pattern lines.

The Pocket Watch design uses several important texturing patterns, the scrubby-line stroke (Squares 61–64), tightly packed spots (Square 56), and the curved-line stroke (Squares 69–70), which can be found in the Creating a Practice Board section on page 41. The crosshatching pattern, whether worked with wide spacing (Squares 15–23) or tight spacing (Squares 24–32), is used in this design for the medium and pale shaded areas of the pocket watch's body.

Tracing: The pattern for The Pocket Watch contains lines for the element outlines as well as guidelines for the five different tonal value areas. These tonal value guidelines are most apparent in the outer ring of the watch. In my sample, I have traced only the element outlines of the pattern. You can also trace the tonal value guidelines if you wish.

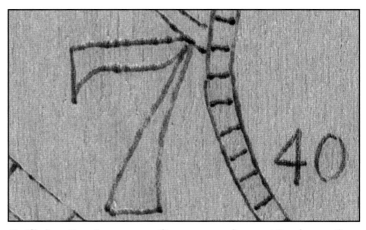

Outlining: Burning your outline on a medium setting keeps the outlining from becoming too dark early in the work. You can re-burn sections of the outlines later to darken them as necessary.

Step 2: Very Dark Tones

The burning for this pattern has been broken down into four tonal values: very dark, dark, medium, and light. Set your thermostat to a medium-high temperature. Use a slow, scrubby-line stroke (Squares 61–64) to fill in the very dark tonal values on your clock. For some of the small areas, you can fill that section by touching the tip of the tool to the wood and then lifting the tip. This burns small tightly packed black spots (Square 56). When using the texture of small dark spots, the closer you pack the spots into the area, the darker that area will become.

Very dark tones: The darkest areas of the watch pattern are the numbers, the triangles on the circular minute dial, the outer ring of the dial, and the inner circle on the seconds dial. There are several areas of very dark shadow in the winding set area, along the left side of the watch body, the watch hands, and in the upper section of the twisted cord. Mark the registration lines on the sides of the cylinder.

Very dark tones (Value #1) map

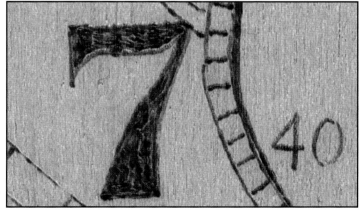

Very dark tones, close-up: The numbers are the most important elements of this design. By burning them to the darkest tonal value, you give them both strength and visual emphasis.

Step 3: Dark Tones

Reduce the temperature slightly and begin working the dark areas. I have used both the scrubby-line fill and a short curved-line fill (Squares 69–70) for my texturing. The burning lines in both of these textures are tightly packed to create the color tone.

Dark tones: This burning of the dark tones includes the remaining portions of the clock hands, a large portion of the left side of the winding stem area and areas in the twisted cord, both above and below the clock, and the tassel. A ring of dark tone shadow goes around the clock body. One small section on the lower left side of the clock body remains unburned.

Dark tones (Value #2) map

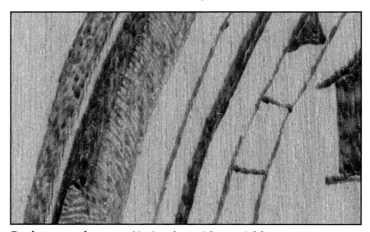

Dark tones, close-up: Notice that with a variable-temperature tool you can completely fill an area, allowing little or no unburned wood to show, using medium-toned coloring. If you are using a one-temperature tool, you may wish to use a wide crosshatch texture (Squares 15–23) in this area, letting some of the wood color show to achieve an overall dark but not black tone.

Step 4: Medium Tones

For the medium-toned values, I have left the temperature setting the same. Use a tight crosshatch pattern (Squares 24–32) that allows some of the original wood coloring to show through the burning to fill in the medium areas.

Medium tones: An inner circle of shading in the clock body, especially in the upper left side is worked using a medium tone. There are also medium-toned areas in the winding stem area, the twisted cord, and the tassel. Notice that there is a section in the clock body's left side adjacent to the clock dial that remains unburned.

Medium tones (Value #3) map

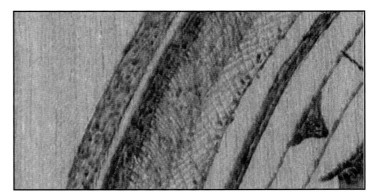

Medium tones, close-up: The temperature setting has not been changed between the dark tone step and the medium tone step. The color changes instead because of the texturing pattern. Crosshatch texturing allows some of the original wood to show through the burned lines, therefore giving a lighter or paler look than tightly packed lines burned at the same temperature. If you are using a one-temperature tool and you crosshatched the dark tones, allow more original wood between your crosshatch burned lines for this step.

Step 5: Light Tones

The temperature setting has been reduced to medium-low. Using a scrubby-line stroke, burn in the light areas. When you have completed the burning, you should have four very distinct color tones in the work with the face of the clock remaining the original color of the wood.

Light tones: A light value is used to fill in the minute ring of the clock dial and the seconds dial, the inner ring on the clock dial, and much of the right side of the clock body. The lower side of the open loop in the winding stem is completed in light value as are the forward sections of the twisted cord.

Light tones (Value #4) map

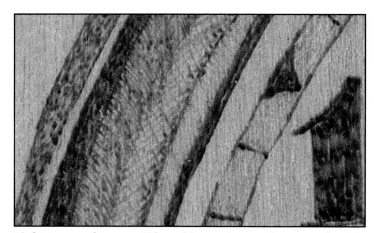

Light tones, close-up: When this step is complete, you should have four distinct tonal values ranging from very dark to light. The background to the clock dial remains unburned. If you are using a one-temperature tool, unplug your tool. Allow it to cool down, and then plug it in again. At that point, burn the light tones before your tool reaches its maximum heat setting.

Step 6: Finishing Steps

Once the burning is complete, lightly sand the surface of the project with fine-grit sandpaper or a foam-core emery board to remove the roughness. Next, use a white artist's eraser over the burning to remove any pencil lines from the original tracing. Set your work where you can look over the project. Check that you have both very dark chocolate areas in the work as well as very pale linen colors to create contrast in the work. Are there middle tones of medium brown and coffee-with-cream shades?

Even though you have worked through the steps of the project, new layering or shading can be added at this point to strengthen your design. This is an excellent time to sign and date your work in the lower right-hand corner. Once any touch-ups are finished, re-sand lightly, dust, and seal your project with either polyurethane or a paste wax (see the Finishing Steps for Woodburning section on page 26 for more information).

Creating a Real Wall Clock

Once you've mastered the tonal values, you may want to create this project as the background of an actual wall clock. Your woodburning becomes the clock face with battery clock hands to keep time.

Step 1: Purchase battery clockworks. Battery clocks come with different lengths of shafts that go through the wood and hold the clock hands. Be sure to match the length of this shaft to the thickness of your wood.

Step 2: Measure the length of the big hand of the battery clock. Then, reduce the size of the burning pattern so that the length of the big hand in the pattern is identical to the length of the battery clock's big hand. This will be an approximate pattern width of 5½" to 6".

Step 3: Trace this small-sized pattern to the plywood, but leave out the hands of the pattern clock. Mark a ¼" margin beyond the outline of the clock.

Step 4: With a scroll saw, cut out the clock along the ¼"-margin line. Drill a hole in the center of the clock that matches the diameter of the battery clock's shaft.

Step 5: Burn the pattern. You might consider adding a manufacturer's name in the clock face area directly under the number 12. Use your surname as the manufacturer (examples: Johnson's Clockworks or Smith's Swiss Movements).

Step 6: Once the burning is complete, mount the battery clock through the hole you drilled.

Part 3

Projects & Patterns

Now that you have mastered the techniques and the theory behind woodburning,

it's time to put your skills to work. In this next part, you'll find three step-by-step

demonstrations. *Dragonette* is a rather simple burning pattern designed for beginners.

In it, you'll use basic woodburning strokes to create several tonal values. *Mallard*

Drake was created for intermediate woodburners. It features more difficult techniques,

a greater number of tonal values, and a colored finish. *The Country Church* was

designed for advanced woodburners. Employing many different texturing techniques

and a wide variety of tonal values gives this landscape piece the illusion of depth.

After you complete each of the demonstrations, you can continue with the rest of the

original woodburning patterns featured in each part. Each design includes a pattern

and a photograph of the finished piece.

Beginning Projects

The *Dragonette* is a wonderful beginner's project that will allow you to experiment with your different tip styles and with the tonal values you can create with your woodburner. Because the *Dragonette* is a mythical creature, this pattern is very adaptable. So, if one area becomes a little lighter or a little darker or if your outlines do not exactly follow the tracing lines, this design will still finish beautifully.

Once you have completed the *Dragonette*, you can move on to the 10 additional beginning designs included in this section. These projects use simple texturing or basic tonal values—perfect for the new woodburner. They include a straight-line textured burning for *Our Daily Bread* and *Goldfish* and quick, negative space designs for *Pentagram Star* and *My Room Gingerbread Man*. The *Wild Rose Corner* shows the use of dramatic tonal contrasts. *Single Briar Rose* and *Summer Morning Sun Face* let you combine basic shading, outlining, and tonal value contrasts.

Creating the *Dragonette* Step-by-Step

Dragonette has claimed a battle shield as his favorite resting spot. With wings flared, he is quite ready to protect his territory. In fact, he is so intense in his attitudes that he has twisted his tail into a Celtic knot. With bold, dark tonal areas contrasting against the original color of the wood in the shield's cross, this pattern makes an excellent beginner's project.

The original design was worked on a 9" by 9" basswood pre-routed wall plaque. The design itself measures 7" by 7". It was burned using a variable-temperature tool and a writing tip; however, this project is very suitable for a one-temperature tool.

Skills List

Tool:	Variable-temperature or one-temperature tool
Tip:	Writing tip or universal tip
Wood:	Pre-routed basswood wall plaque, 9" x 9"

Textures: Short curved line (Square 70)
Long curved line (Square 69)
Random curls (Squares 33–37)
Scrubby line (Squares 61–64)
Long scales (Square 57
Dash stroke (Squares 1–5)

Tonal Values for *Dragonette*

Dragonette

© Lora S. Irish

Trace the pattern onto the wood using vellum or onionskin tracing paper and graphite pencils.

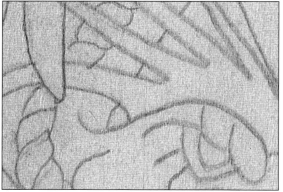

Clean up smudges with a white artist's eraser.

Step 1–6: Transferring the pattern

Step 1: Begin the work by lightly sanding the wood with fine-grit sandpaper.

Step 2: Remove any sanding dust with a lint-free cloth or a drafter's dusting brush.

Step 3: Make a copy of the pattern from this book on vellum or onionskin tracing paper.

Step 4: Rub the back of the tracing paper with a soft #4B to #6B pencil until you have created a dark, even layer of graphite.

Step 5: Tape the paper to your board, graphite side down, and retrace the pattern lines. Trace only those lines that you need to guide you through the work.

Step 6: With a white artist's eraser, rub off any smudges or streaks left during the tracing process.

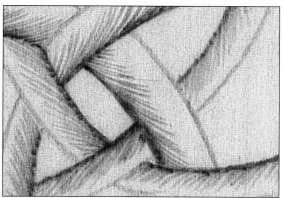

Here, one side of the dragon's body is shaded with short curved lines.

Step 7–10: Shading one side of the body

Step 7: Begin the project by shading the top portion of the dragonette's body where it disappears under the front wing. Use a medium temperature setting and a short curved-line stroke (Square 70).

Step 8: As the body flows down the plaque, the shaded side will become the bottom portion of the body where the tail twists under the shield. Limit the shading to the bottom side of the tail when it reappears on the right side of the shield.

Step 9: Follow this side as the tail travels through the knot, whether that side is on the top or bottom of the dragonette's body. Stop the shading where the tail feathers begin.

Step 10: When the short curved-line shading is complete, add an outline along that side of the dragon's body and tail.

Be sure to shade the correct side of the tail as it twists and turns.

Step 11–12: Shading the remaining body

Step 11: Repeat the shading steps for the remaining side of the dragonette's body. Notice how the short curved-line stroke for this side follows the direction established when you worked the first side. The curved lines from the two sides work toward each other, creating a broken S-shaped line.

Step 12: When the shading is complete, add an outline to the second side of the body.

Now, shade the other side of the dragon's body.

It is much easier to shade this half of the dragon's body now that the other side is done.

Step 13–15: Belly-fold shading

Step 13: As with the body, the belly folds will be worked in two phases, one side at a time.

Step 14: Begin your work where the neck joins the head. Shade on the lower outside edge of the belly fold. This shading is created with short, curved lines that radiate from the lower, outer point.

Step 15: As you work through the belly folds, limit the shading to the lower portion for each new fold.

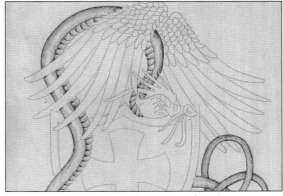

The belly-fold shading has been completed.

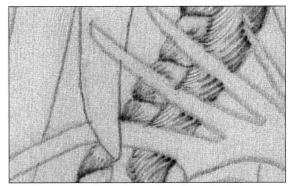

Use short curved lines that radiate from the lower outer point of the belly fold.

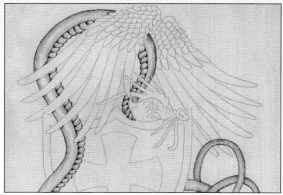

Burn a dark triangle wherever the belly fold meets the body.

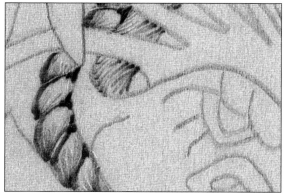

Burn the dark triangles using a medium-high setting to emphasize the separation of the belly folds.

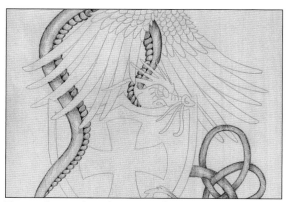

The random curl stroke creates the wings' shadows to the body.

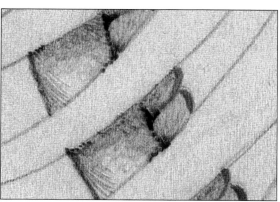

The texture here is delicate but important for realism.

Step 16–18: Belly shading for the remaining side

Step 16: The second stage of the belly shading is worked where the belly fold meets the body. Use a medium-high heat setting.

Step 17: In this angled area, burn a small, very dark, triangle shape. This separates the top section of one belly fold from the bottom section of the next belly fold. Because this triangle is worked to a darker tone, it pushes the belly fold deeply into its junction with the body.

Step 18: Add a dark, comma-shaped line along the outside edge of each belly fold. Do not completely outline these folds; you are just accenting them.

Step 19–20: Adding wing shadows to the body

Step 19: On a medium temperature setting and using a random curl stroke (Squares 33–37), add a light layering of shadow to the body beneath each wing feather. This light shadowing implies that the wing lies over the body and therefore casts a shadow on that part of the body.

Step 20: Shadowed areas appear on the body on both sides of the wing's shoulder and beneath the five long wing feathers using the random curl stroke.

Step 21–33: Detailing the face

Step 21: The shading in the face is done with short curved lines. Set the tool to a medium temperature. Then, shade the nose ridges working from the left top.

Step 22: Shade the upper eye ridges and the nostril area starting at the bottom left.

Step 23: Burn the folds to the left of the eye with the short lines close to the eye.

Step 24: Start curved lines at the mouth area where the chin and jaw rest on the shield and pull them upward, arching to the left.

Step 25: Fill the nose tendrils with light-toned, long curved lines that follow the direction of that tendril.

Step 26: Work the crest with long curved lines that start at the skull and flow to the points of the crest.

Step 27: When the shading is complete, turn the temperature up slightly. Add a separating line between each nose ridge.

Step 28: Outline the bottom edge of the upper eye ridges.

Step 29: Use a large comma stroke to create the nostril.

Step 30: Detail along the lip line of the mouth and along the jaw line.

Step 31: Increase the temperature; then, add the mouth with a short scrubby-line stroke.

Step 32: Texture the eye with the same stroke, leaving a small white area for the eye's highlight.

Step 33: The folds to the left of the eye are darkly detailed, and a small spot of darkness is added to the inside corner of the eye.

Step 34–35: Long wing feathers

Step 34: For the feathering of the wings, turn your tool to a hot temperature. Working the long front wing feather, use a curved-line stroke that starts on the outside edge of the feather and flows upward toward the inside edge. A dark starting point will appear naturally along this outer edge.

Step 35: The long back wing feathers are worked in the same manner, but turn the tool temperature down to a medium setting.

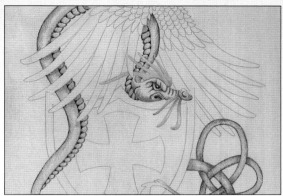

Shade the face and facial hair with short curved lines.

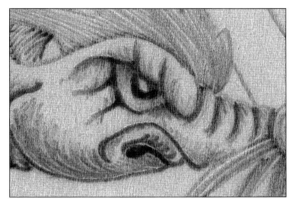

The mouth, pupil, nostrils, and deep creases along the eye should be the darkest values on the face.

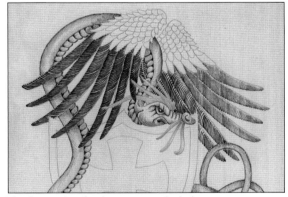

The front wing feathers are much darker than the back wing feathers.

Start the stroke from the edge of the feather and curve inward.

Re-burning the feathers surrounding the dragon's neck and face will emphasize the border there.

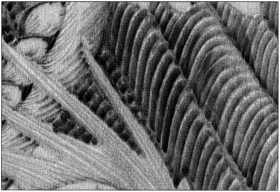

Burning a second layer will subtly darken the area.

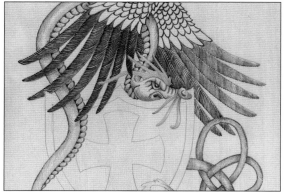

Outline the shoulder feathers.

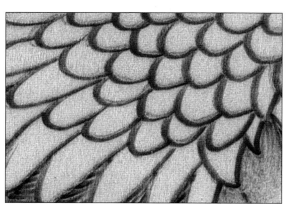

Use a high temperature to burn the outline; the dark line will be needed later.

Step 36: Adding a second layer to the back wing

Step 36: After the long back wing feathers are completed, add a second layer in the area of the wing directly behind the dragonette's face and neck. Lay the tool tip back into the already burned curved line and re-burn that line. This will lightly darken this area of the wing to create more contrast between the wing and the face.

Step 37: Outlining the shoulder feathers

Step 37: Setting the tool tip to a high temperature, outline each of the shoulder feathers.

Step 38–41: Burning the shoulder feathers and tail

Step 38: Keep the tool on a high setting and use a short scrubby-line stroke (Squares 61–64) to shade the top section of each shoulder feather. Because the scrubby-line stroke is applied at a slightly faster pace, this shadowing will become slightly paler than the slowly burned outline of the previous step.

Step 39: Outline each individual feather in the shoulder area using high heat and a long fish-scale texture (Square 57).

Step 40: Turn the tool temperature down slightly to a medium-high setting. Working from the right side of the tail tip, pull long curved lines through the tail tip toward the left side.

Step 41: Outline both sides of the tail tip.

Use the short scrubby-line stroke to shade each individual shoulder feather.

The dark outline from the previous section guides the placement of the scrubby-line shading.

Step 42–43: Shading the body of the shield

Step 42: The mid-ground area of the shield will be worked in two stages. On a medium-high setting, first outline the center cross design in the shield.

Step 43: A random curl stroke (Squares 33–37) is used next to fill in the area of the shield between the central cross design and the outer border of the shield. This random curl stroke will have lots of variations in color tones, giving this area of the shield extra interest.

Outline the cross and use the random curl stroke to fill the inner shield.

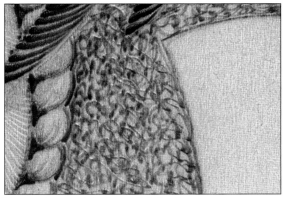

The random curl stroke adds lots of variation in color tones.

The outer border of the shield has been filled with a dash stroke and another layer of texture has been burned onto the outer parts of the inner shield.

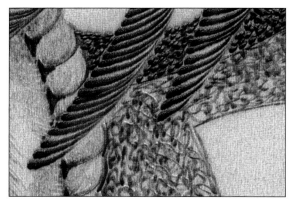

The dark value of the dash stroke adds contrast between the beige of the cross and the shifting value of the shield.

The finished *Dragonette*.

Step 44–46: Adding extra layering to the shield

Step 44: Notice in the photo that the area along the top section and the right side of the shield is darker than the rest of this area. These darker sections require a second layering of the random curl stroke.

Step 45: In both the left and right corners of this mid-ground, add a third layer of work. These added layers give the shield its bowed effect.

Step 46: Turn the tool setting to high and, using a dash stroke (Squares 1–5), fill in the outer border with a very dark color tone. Work this outer border with very tightly packed strokes until it has a solid black or dark chocolate coloring.

Step 47–52: Finishing

Step 47: When the burning is complete, lightly sand the surface of the project with fine-grit sandpaper or a foam-core emery board to remove the roughness.

Step 48: Next, rub a white artist's eraser over the burning to remove any pencil lines from the original tracing.

Step 49: Remove any dust or eraser particles with a lint-free cloth or a drafter's dusting brush.

Step 50: Set your work where you can look over the project. Check that you have very dark chocolate areas as well as very pale linen colors to create contrast in the work. Are there middle tones of medium brown and coffee-with-cream shades? Even though you have worked through the steps of this project, new layering or shading can be added at this point to strengthen your design.

Step 51: This is an excellent time to sign and date your work in the lower right-hand corner.

Step 52: Once any touch-ups are finished, re-sand lightly, dust with a lint-free cloth, and seal your project with either polyurethane or a paste wax.

Dragonette Chessboard

Here is the same *Dragonette* design that you just worked but patterned for a game board or chessboard. The Celtic knot tail design has been increased to include a Celtic knot between the opposing dragonettes. Because this piece was worked on birch plywood, a harder wood than basswood, the tonal values are lighter than the deep color tones created on the *Dragonette* plaque. The width of each burned line tends to be slightly thinner on a harder wood than the width of a line done on a softer wood.

This *Dragonette Chessboard* was worked using the same step-by-step process as the *Dragonette* (with the shield). When the dragons were completed, the dark borderline surrounding the chessboard was burned in the same fashion as the dark borderline of the *Dragonette* (with the shield). The dark squares on the chessboard were burned on a medium setting using tight-spaced crosshatch (Squares 24–32).

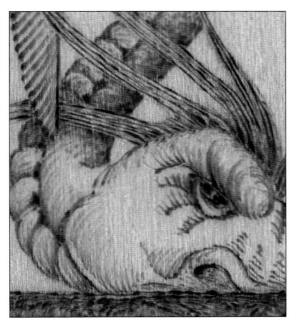

This adaptation of the *Dragonette* pattern has a straight line under the dragon's head.

The *Dragonette Chessboard* features tight-spaced crosshatch on the dark squares.

Make the chessboard come alive with watercolors.

Dragonette Chessboard with Coloring

When the burning for this chessboard was completed and the work sanded, I used watercolors to add bright colors (see larger photo and pattern on page 105). The watercolors were first placed on a glass tile or plate and then were thinned with water until they were fairly transparent. The paints were then applied using soft sable brushes by floating a light coat on each area. One color can be laid over another color to create shading or to deepen the original color. Be sure to allow the first layering of color to dry well before adding more. Any mistakes can easily be lifted with a wet brush.

Step 1: Begin by applying one coat of the highlight color throughout the entire designated area. Do all of the highlight colors at one time. Allow the work to dry well, about one half hour.

Step 2: Where one element of a design goes underneath a second element, the first element will have a shadow area. Add the shading color to these areas of the design. Allow the highlight colors to remain unworked in the areas of the element that are farther removed from an overlapping element.

Step 3: In any small, tight areas where one element tucks under another, add one more layer of the dark shading color. For instance, for any one loop in the dragonette's body where both ends of that loop tuck under another element, you will have a small section of dark shading color, a wider section of shading color, a large area of highlight color, then back to the shading and dark shading colors.

Step 4: Once all of the coloring has been applied, allow the board to dry overnight. Then, give the chessboard several light coats of spray polyurethane. Two holes can be drilled along the top edge of the plywood board to string a leather handle for hanging. Now your chessboard can decorate your wall when it is not being used for your latest game of chess.

Dragonette Chessboard **Color Chart**

Most areas of this design will use two different colors to create the final effect. The first color, the highlight color, is applied to establish the general color of the entire element's area. For example, the entire face and body of the dragonette is first painted with yellow ochre. Once this highlight color has dried, a second color, called the shading color, is applied to any area of the element that tucks under or touches an adjacent area. For example, the neck of the dragonette is shaded with verde green where the neck touches the base of the head. The neck is also shaded with verde green where it tucks under the wings.

Area	Highlight Color	Shading Color
Body and face	Yellow ochre	Verde green
Tail tip	Deep yellow	Yellow ochre
Long wing feathers	Verde green	Light turquoise
Wing shoulders	Verde green	Light turquoise
Celtic knot line	Yellow ochre	Burnt sienna
Shadowing for all areas		Raw umber
Dark squares		Raw umber
Light squares		50% yellow ochre and 50% burnt sienna mixed half and half

Dragonette Chessboard

© Lora S. Irish

Our Daily Bread

© Lora S. Irish

Goldfish

© Lora S. Irish

Ivy Line

© Lora S. Irish

© Lora S. Irish

My Room Gingerbread Man

© Lora S. Irish

Single Briar Rose

© Lora S. Irish

© Lora S. Irish

Pentagram Star

© Lora S. Irish

Intermediate Projects

The *Mallard Drake* is a realistic pattern, so tonal values and contrast become much more important than in the *Dragonette* design. As we work through this step-by-step, pay special attention to establishing definite light, medium, and dark tones. Again, variations in your burned value tones may vary from those shown here depending on your tool tip and woodburner style. The focus of this project is on learning how to create contrasts for different areas of the work.

Once you have mastered creating multiple contrasting values and shading by woodburning *Mallard Drake*, you are ready for the *Buffalo Skull Dream Weaver Circle* and the *Solar Flare Sun Face*, both of which incorporate a wide variety of textures and tones. *Old-Timer Fireman* and *New York's Finest* let you practice the human face, while *Western Horse*, *American Eagle*, and *White-Tailed Deer Lodge* are examples of the wildlife portraits you will be ready to work. The intermediate section also includes *Berry Green Man* and *Oak Man*, two popular themes that combine the human face and nature.

Creating the *Mallard Drake Step-by-Step*

This mallard drake, with his beautifully colored wings, green head, and rust chest, is captured in front of a graceful stand of autumn cattails. The three-dimensional look of the duck is created through tonal value textures. When the burning is completed, coloring can be added using artist-quality colored pencils. The original burning was done on birch plywood and measures 11" by 6½".

Before you begin, read through all of the steps. Notice that every section of the project is worked from back to front or from bottom to top. This process allows you more control over each section: It is much easier to lay an area of detailing over the pattern outlines of an already burned area than it is to cut in a background area around an already burned foreground element. In the *Mallard Drake*, the highest foreground element is the wing's shoulder area, the last area to be worked.

Because the entire *Mallard Drake* was created using curved lines (Squares 69–70); half circles, a variation of scales (Square 48); dash strokes (Squares 1–5); and straight-line strokes (Square 66–68); you will want to choose a new texture for the cattail leaves and heads. I chose the random curl stroke (Squares 33–37). By changing the texture pattern, you are visually stating that this element is different. In this project, the random curl lines show that this area of the work features leaves, not feathers. For the cattail heads, a dash stroke creates the black-chocolate coloring. To keep these areas different from the dash stroke areas of the mallard, I worked the spots in a different direction—up to down instead of side to side.

This project was worked using the variable-temperature tool with the writing tip on birch plywood. If you are working with the one-temperature tool, please use the universal tip. Heat settings are noted for each step of this project, so please refer back to the Using Shading and Texture section, beginning on page 32, for more information.

As you burn this intermediate project, you'll see that it really is no harder to create than the beginner's project—there are just more steps!

Skills List

Tool:	Variable-temperature or one-temperature tool
Tip:	Writing tip or universal tip
Wood:	Birch plywood, 11" x 6½"
Textures:	Curved lines (Squares 69–70)
	Scales (Square 48)
	Random curls (Squares 33–37)
	Dash stroke (Squares 1–5)
	Straight line (Squares 66–68)
	Tightly packed spots (Square 56)
	Scrubby-line stroke (Squares 61–64)

Tonal Values

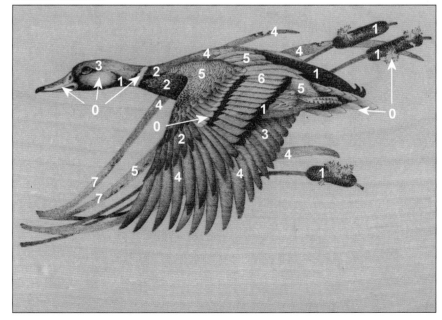

Mallard Drake

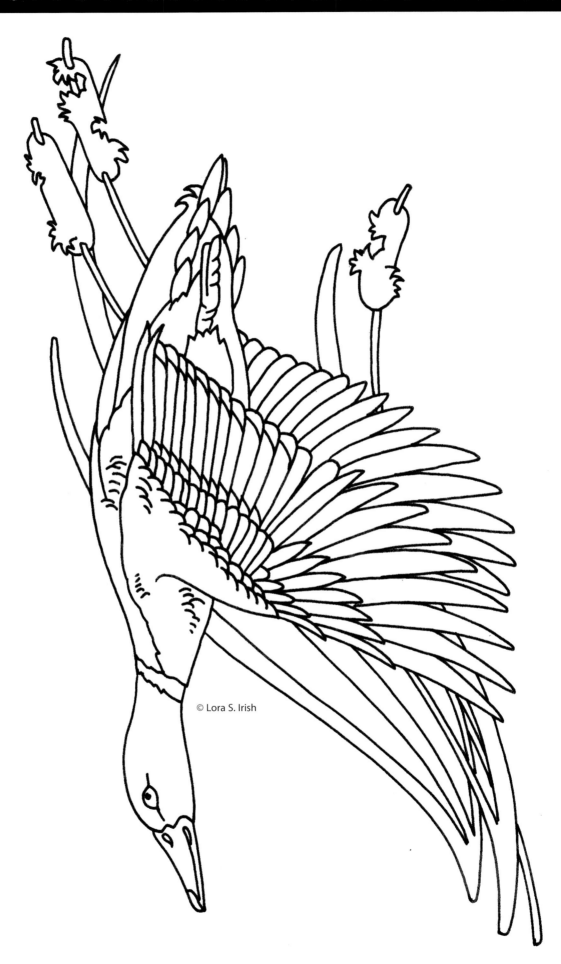

© Lora S. Irish

Using a cool or medium-cool setting, trace the outline of the bird and the wing feathers.

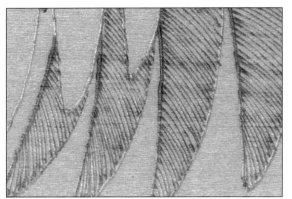

Use curved-line strokes to fill the back wing feathers.

The second layer of burning on the back wing creates dimension.

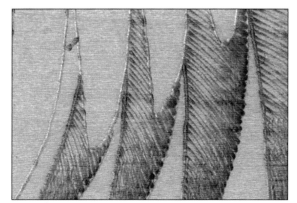

You may find it easier to re-burn the back wing by turning the project upside down.

Step 1–6: Transferring the pattern, pale outlining

Step 1: Begin by lightly sanding your plywood with fine-grit sandpaper. Remove any dust with a lint-free cloth or a drafter's dusting brush.

Step 2: Make a copy of the pattern from this book on vellum or onionskin tracing paper. Rub the back of the tracing paper with a soft pencil until you have created a dark, even layer of graphite.

Step 3: Tape the pattern paper to your board and retrace the pattern lines using a hard #H to #2B pencil or ink pen. Trace only those lines that you need to guide you through the work.

Step 4: With a white artist's eraser, rub off any smudges or streaks left during the tracing process.

Step 5: Set your tool to a cool or medium-cool setting; outline the pattern lines. You want this outlining to be a soft, caramel color. You can darken any outline to give it more strength after the tones and shading have been completed. Notice that the outer edge of each long flight feather in both the front and back wings and the large tail feathers are included in this outlining step. Do not burn the small shoulder feathers at this time.

Step 6: Leave your thermostat on the cool or medium-cool setting. Start burning the back wing feathers. These feathers are worked in two layers of burning. For the first layer, pull curved-line strokes (Squares 69–70) into each wing feather. Allow some spacing between the lines so that some of the original wood coloring shows. Each curved line has a downward motion and is worked from the front edge of the feather to the back edge. The inside coloring of the mallard's wings is a light beige tone, so you will want this wing area burned to a paler tonal value than you will be burning the front wing.

Step 7–8: The back wing

Step 7: When the first layer of burning on the feathers has been completed, turn the project board upside down and begin your second layer of burning.

Step 8: For this layer, lay the tip into one of the already burned curved lines, starting the stroke on the back edge of the feather. Pull the curved line halfway into the wing's thickness to make the back half of the feather darker than the front half. (When finished, you will have done a second layering of burning on the curved lines, but only on one-half of the first burned lines.)

Step 9–10: Russet breast and tail underside

Step 9: The breast area and the tail's underside are both very dark on the drake. Turn your temperature setting to medium-high and use a dash stroke (Squares 1–5) to fill these areas with dark spotting. Notice on the close-up photo that the dashes at the top of the breast allow some wood color to show through, and then the dashes become more tightly packed as they move away from this highlighted area toward the wing shoulder.

Step 10: The tail's tip is filled with tightly packed dashes to create a black-chocolate coloring.

Fill the duck's breast with a dash stroke.

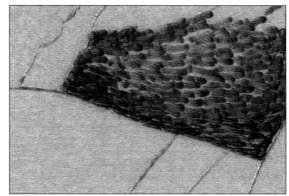
Make the dash stroke closer together toward the shoulder and the bottom of the breast.

Step 11–16: Underbelly & undersides of tail feathers

Step 11: The underbelly of the drake has the same beige-to-cream coloring as the inside of the wings. This area needs a pale tonal value, so set your thermostat to a cool-medium setting.

Step 12: Use a scrubby-line stroke (Squares 61–64) to work this area. Notice the highlight area that was left unburned in the underbelly just above the leg.

Step 13: Add a second layer of scrubby-line strokes where the underbelly touches the wing, both above and below the leg. This second layering adds a light shadow to the belly.

Step 14: Work the undersides of the tail feathers in straight-line strokes that start at the front of each feather. These lines are pulled to about one-half the feather's length (see Steps 9–10 for the close-up of the undersides of the tail feathers).

Step 15: Because the back wing is behind the underbelly of the duck's body, it needs a small amount of dark shadowing to tuck it under the body.

Step 16: Turn your setting up to a medium temperature and re-burn the curved-line strokes in this wing area just under the underbelly. Darken this thin section of wing to a medium tonal value.

Use scrubby lines to fill the underbelly and undersides of the tail feathers.

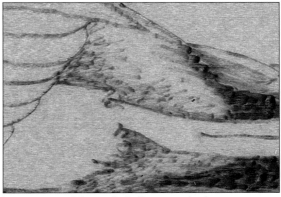
Leave some of the underbelly untouched.

Use the scrubby-line stroke again to shade the forward section of the back.

Step 17–19: Forward section of the back

Step 17: Burn the forward section of the duck's back on a medium setting using the scrubby-line stroke.

Step 18: Place the highlight area for this section where the back begins to disappear behind the top of the front wing. Use wider-spaced scrubby lines in this area.

Step 19: Add a second layer of scrubby-line strokes to the front section of the duck's back where it touches the neckband.

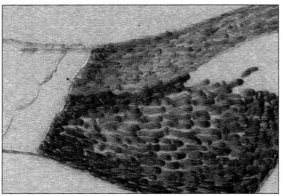

The forward section of the back is lighter than the breast.

Shade the upper tail section using tightly packed spots.

Step 20–21: Upper tail section

Step 20: Using a medium-high setting and tightly packed spots (Square 56), fill the remaining portion of the mallard's back. This is the upper tail section.

Step 21: Burn this area to an even black-chocolate tone.

This section of the tail should be burned to a black-chocolate tone.

Step 22–23: Shading the head

Step 22: The head of the mallard drake has a distinct shape. The head and neck area are curved like the back of a bowl with a second small bowl where the duck's cheek lies. This means that this area of the burning needs shading to create the two distinct rounded areas. With your tool setting still on medium-high and using tightly packed spots, fill in the darkly shadowed areas, as shown in the close-up photo, to a black-chocolate value.

Step 23: Also burn the nostrils, mouth corner, and bill tip at this time.

Use tightly packed spots to shape the mallard's distinctive head shading.

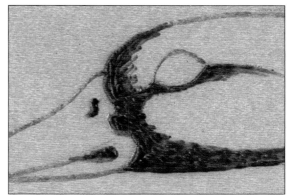

The nostril, tip of the bill, mouth, and facial shading should be some of the darkest values on the duck.

Step 24–26: Mid-tone shading for the face

Step 24: First note that there are two areas of highlight in the mallard's head and neck area. One is directly behind the eye; this highlights the first bowl area of the head. The second is in the center of his cheek, which highlights the smaller bowl area.

Step 25: Work a medium-high setting of scrubby-line strokes in these areas, allowing the stroke to become more widely spaced as you reach the highlights.

Step 26: Add a second layer of scrubby-line strokes along the bill and head to blend the dark and medium tones of shading.

The scrubby-line stroke will add a second value to the head.

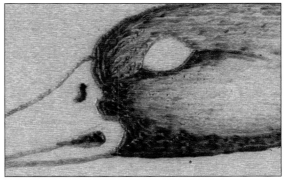

As you get nearer the highlights behind the eye and the cheek, lighten your strokes.

The eye has been shaded to a caramel color using tightly packed spots.

Step 27–31: The eye

Step 27: Again, look for the highlight of the eye. This is an area that you will not be burning.

Step 28: Work a medium-high setting of scrubby-line strokes to the eye to create a medium, caramel coloring.

Step 29: Add a second layer of burning to the eye using tightly packed spots in the upper section.

Step 30: A black-chocolate outline is added to the lower eyelid. Now, most likely, the entire eye has some woodburning color.

Step 31: To create the fine line of white at the bottom of the eye and to emphasize the eye's highlight, use a woodcarver's round gouge to carefully carve away a fine sliver of wood in these areas.

If necessary, delineate the eye from the crease beneath it using a woodcarver's round gouge.

Shade the top of the bill with short straight-line strokes.

Step 32–35: Shading the bill

Step 32: The mallard's bill uses short straight-line fill strokes on a medium-high setting to create the dark patch of coloring along the top of the bill.

Step 33: Shade the bottom section of the bill in the same way.

Step 34: Add a very small amount of detailing around the bill's nostril.

Step 35: Outline the foot while the tool is on the medium-high setting. Notice that, on the drake, these two areas—the beak and the feet—are the only areas completely outlined. This distinguishes these two areas from the feathering of the duck's body.

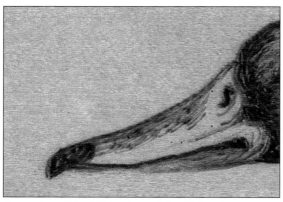

The center of the bill has been left a high value.

Step 36–38: Upper front wing feathers

Step 36: A set of four long feathers rests at the top of the drake's wing. These feathers are above the colored feathers and lie over the mallard's back. Detail them using a widely spaced curved-line stroke and a medium temperature setting.

Step 37: Work the curved lines from the bottom of the feather, pulling toward the top of the feather.

Step 38: Fill in one-half of each feather.

Detail the upper front wing feathers with a widely spaced curved-line stroke.

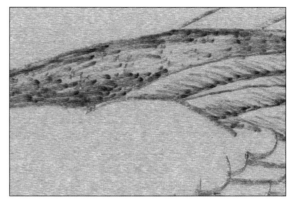

Use a medium temperature setting to shade the bottom half of the feathers.

Step 39–42: Outer grouping of front wing feathers

Step 39: The grouping of long feathers on the outside back edge of the front wing is worked next. These wing feathers will be worked in three layers.

Step 40: The first layer is done exactly as the back wing was worked in Steps 7–8.

Step 41: Reduce the setting on your thermostat to a medium-cool setting.

Step 42: Starting on the front side of each feather, pull a curved-line stroke across the full length. Curve downward as you burn. The curved lines in this first layer are widely spaced.

Shade the outer grouping of front wing feathers.

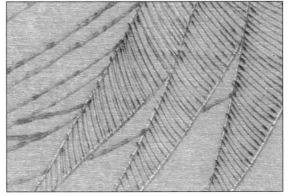

The curved-line stroke is pulled across the full width of the feather.

The second and third layers of the flight feathers.

Step 43–44: Flight feather details

Step 43: The lower section of long feathers on the wing that was just worked contains the longest flight feathers. Turn your project board upside down, and starting at the back of the feather and working a line one-half of the way into the feather, re-burn the curved lines. This will make the outer back edge of each feather darker than the front side.

Step 44: Burn a third layering one-quarter of the way into each feather to make black-chocolate tips on this grouping of flight feathers.

Create black-chocolate tips on the flight feathers.

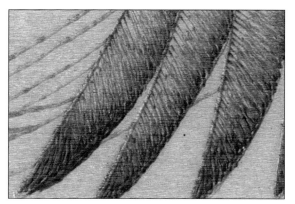

Burn a second layer of lines to lessen the contrast between the back and middle wing feathers.

Step 45–46: Coloring wing feathers

Step 45: The section of wing feathers above the flight feathers is the next group of feathers to be worked. To create a blending between these feathers and the darker flight feathers, add a second layer of curved-line strokes to the first four lower feathers of this group. Work this layer over one-half of the feather's width.

Step 46: When you are finished, you will have a grouping of dark flight feathers, four medium-toned colored feathers, and an upper section of colored feathers that remains pale in value.

The contrast between the two sections is not as bold as it once was.

Step 47: Dark half circles on colored feathers

Step 47: The colored feathers of the mallard's wing have two dark half-circle sections: one at the top and one at the bottom of each feather. These are burned on a medium-high setting using tightly packed spots. You want to achieve a black-chocolate coloring for these areas.

Use tightly packed spots to create two bars on the mallard's wing.

The black-chocolate bars are very dark in value.

Step 48: Short flight feathers

Step 48: Above the long flight feathers in the front wing are two groups of shorter flight feathers. These two groups are worked exactly the same as the long flight feathers in Steps 43–44, but with the thermostat set to a medium-high heat.

In the same way as you did the long flight feathers, shade the short flight feathers.

Use a touch-and-lift stroke to shade the feathers.

Use a curved stroke to burn the row of feathers immediately above the bar.

Be sure to leave white tips on the ends of these feathers.

Cover the wing shoulder with small, tightly packed scales.

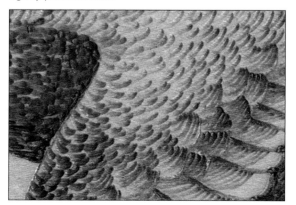

Notice the second layer of scales near the bottom part of the shoulder.

Step 49: Upper colored feathers

Step 49: Above the colored feathers that have already been worked in Steps 45–46, there is a second grouping of colored feathers. Each feather in this group has a white tip that will not be burned. Following the same direction of flow that you used on the first group of colored feathers, use a medium-high setting and the curved-line stroke to accent the upper section of each of these feathers.

Step 50–54: Wing shoulder

Step 50: Set your temperature to a medium setting.

Step 51: Burn small, tightly packed scales (these are just small half circles) to create the edges of the small round feathers that cover the shoulder. You can see in the close-up that these do not need to be complete half circles or touch any other half circle. Keep the burning strokes long and flowing.

Step 52: Re-burn a second layer of half circles on the front lower section of the shoulder to darken this area.

Step 53: The highlight area of the shoulder, the area where you will widely space the half circles, is at the top front of the shoulder.

Step 54: The neckband, which is a circle of white feathers between the green head and the russet breast of the drake, remains unburned.

Step 55–58: Cattail leaves

Step 55: Fill all of the leaves and stems with the random curl stroke. Use a medium setting.

Step 56: Add a second layer of random curls to any section of the leaf that goes under another element, either under the mallard or under another leaf.

Step 57: A third layer was added to the stems to dramatically darken these areas.

Step 58: A few tightly packed spots were burned where the leaves have torn holes.

Fill the cattail leaves with a random curl stroke.

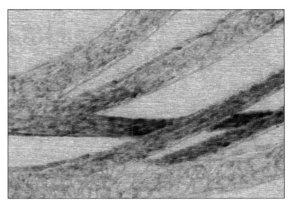

Any leaves that go under another element should be darkened to add dimension.

Step 59–61: Cattail heads

Step 59: Burn the cattail heads using tightly packed spots on a high setting. Notice the highlight area that runs through the center of each head.

Step 60: The fuzzy fibers of the cattail heads are medium-setting, thin, curved lines. Work these from the head area outward.

Step 61: Add a small black dot at the end of each fuzzy fiber.

Burn the cattail heads on a high temperature using tightly packed spots.

Be sure to leave a highlight area in the middle of each head.

The finished *Mallard Drake.*

Step 62–68: Finishing

Step 62: When the burning is complete, lightly sand the surface of the project with fine-grit sandpaper or a foam-core emery board to remove the roughness.

Step 63: Next, rub a white artist's eraser over the burning to remove any pencil lines from the original tracing.

Step 64: Remove any dust and eraser particles with a lint-free cloth or a large drafter's dusting brush.

Step 65: Set your work where you can look over the project. Check that you have very dark chocolate areas as well as very pale linen colors to create contrast in the work. Are there middle tones of medium brown and coffee-with-cream shades? Does your mallard have a three-dimensional feeling? Even though you have worked through the steps of this project, new layering or shading can be added at this point to strengthen your design.

Step 66: This is an excellent time to sign and date your work in the lower right-hand corner.

Step 67: Once any touch-ups are finished, re-sand lightly, dust, and seal your project with either polyurethane or a paste wax if you want the project to remain in its woodburned form.

Step 68: If you want to add coloring, go on to Steps 69–74.

Step 69–74: Colored pencil work

Step 69: Artist-quality colored pencils are my favorite way to add coloring to a woodburning. They require no mixing, no special media, and no clean-up steps. Of the three types of colored pencils—regular, oil, and watercolor—I used the regular dry pencils for this piece. Keep the pencils very sharp as you work; resharpen often.

Step 70: Apply the colored pencils in very light layers. Four to five layers of color are needed to create a nice, rich color tone. By using light layers, the wax and chalk content of the pencils does not become cloudy or milky-looking over your woodburning's tonal values.

Step 71: Use a soft pressure as you apply the pencil color. Do not force the pencil point into the woodburned strokes; instead, let the color lie on the high ridges between those strokes.

Step 72: Colors can be mixed by applying one color over another. For example, a light color of burnt sienna applied over several coats of pale yellow will create a light burnt orange.

Step 73: Use the color chart below as a guide to coloring the *Mallard Drake*. Apply white to the lower line in the eye, the neckband, the upper colored wing feathers, the upper wing feather group of four, the belly, the tail feathers, the inside back wing, and the fuzzy fibers of the cattail heads.

Step 74: When the pencil coloring is complete, give the woodburning several light coats of spray polyurethane to both protect the wood and seal in the color work.

Colored pencil can add flair to your finished woodburning.

Allow the pencil to skim over the top of the burning—do not force the point into the woodburned strokes.

Mallard Drake Color Chart

Area	Highlight Color	Shading Color	Dark Shading Color
Bill	Pale yellow	Yellow ochre	
Head and Neck	Pale yellow	True green	Dark green
Breast	Light burnt sienna	Burnt sienna	Burnt umber
Upper Front Back	Light burnt sienna		
Flight Feathers	Medium brown	Burnt umber	
Shoulder Feathers	White	Pale gray	Blue
Colored Wing Feathers	Light blue	Medium turquoise	Dark purple
Cattail Leaves	Pale yellow	Yellow ochre	Light burnt sienna
Foot	Pale yellow		

Buffalo Skull Dream Weaver Circle

© Lora S. Irish

Western Horse

© Lora S. Irish

New York's Finest

© Lora S. Irish

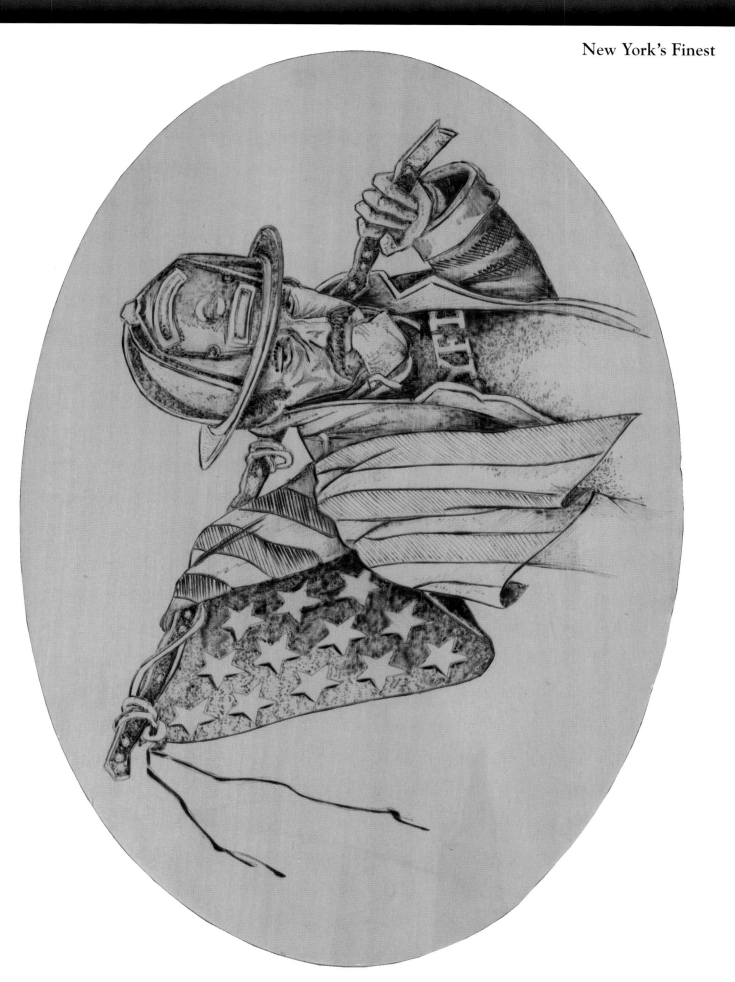

Old-Timer Fireman

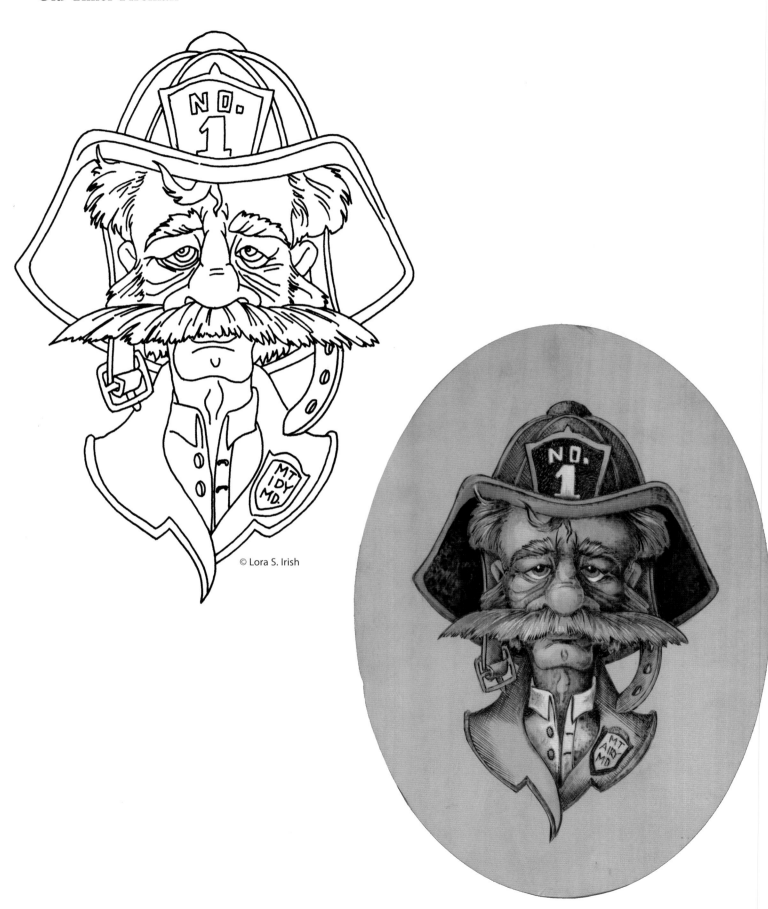

© Lora S. Irish

© Lora S. Irish

Mule Deer Portrait

© Lora S. Irish

White-Tailed Deer Lodge

© Lora S. Irish

American Eagle

© Lora S. Irish

Berry Green Man

© Lora S. Irish

Oak Man

© Lora S. Irish

Advanced Projects

For our advanced project, we will focus on a variety of texture strokes that can be used within a pattern or scene to create tonal values and shape. Texture strokes can be used to show a difference between one element and another. For example, the pine trees in this scene use one texture—the dash stroke—to create needles, while the oak trees use a scrubby line texture. Both are trees, and both are located in the background. The use of texture strokes, however, easily distinguishes the pines from the oak trees. How many layers of texture strokes or how hot of a heat setting will establish the changes in the tonal values of this church scene.

The advanced patterns that follow *The Country Church* focus on control of the shading and highlighting tonal values and the detailing and layering of textures in a design. Fine-line detailing accents these patterns, as shown in *Cowboy Boots, The Philadelphia Derringer,* and *Hide 'n Seek.* The dramatic contrast of tones found in *The End of the Road, Grandpa's Pride and Joy,* and *Harrisburg Star Barn* are done using both texture and temperature to create outstanding black areas against stark white tones. *Horned Owl, Our Town Mantel,* and *Church Mantel* will let you explore the use of all of the techniques you have learned from this book.

Creating *The Country Church* Step-by-Step

This realistic landscape scene features a small country church nestled in an old grove of pines. Early spring or late fall are implied because of the minimal number of leaves on the tall oak trees. Leading up to the church is a stepping stone path that is surrounded by tall, growing grasses. This project has been burned on white birch plywood and measures 8" wide by 6½" tall. As you work through the steps to create this country church, you will be changing the temperature settings on your thermostat. This burning was done using the writing tip.

The practice project in this chapter was worked using the variable-temperature tool with the writing tip on birch plywood. If you are working with the one-temperature tool, please use the universal tip. Heat settings are noted for each step of this project, so please refer back to the Using Shading and Texture section, beginning on page 32, for more information.

Skills List

Tool:	Variable temperature or one-temperature tool
Tip:	Writing tip or universal tip
Wood:	White birch plywood, 8" x 6½"
Textures:	Dash stroke (Squares 1–5)
	Scrubby lines (Squares 61–64)
	Random curls (Squares 33–37)
	Random zigzags (Square 40)
	Straight lines (Squares 66–68)
	Curved lines (Squares 69–70)

Tonal Values

The Country Church

© Lora S. Irish

Transfer the pattern onto the wood with vellum or onionskin paper and graphite.

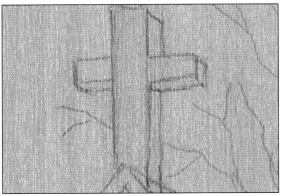

Be sure to erase any smudges with a white artist's eraser.

Step 1–6: Transferring the pattern

Step 1: Begin the work by lightly sanding your plywood with fine-grit sandpaper.

Step 2: Remove any sanding dust with a lint-free cloth or a large drafter's dusting brush.

Step 3: Make a copy of the pattern from the book on vellum or onionskin tracing paper.

Step 4: Rub the back of the tracing paper with a soft pencil, #4B to #6B, until you have created a dark, even layer of graphite.

Step 5: Tape the pattern paper to your board and retrace the pattern lines. Trace only those lines that you need to guide you through the work.

Step 6: With a white artist's eraser, rub off any smudges or streaks left during the tracing process.

Step 7–13: Large background pines and oak trees

Step 7: This pattern will be worked from the background to the foreground, starting with the tall pines and trees behind the church. Use the writing tip at a medium-high temperature setting.

Step 8: The first area to be burned is the background, which includes the large dark-toned pine trees and the two dark deciduous oak trees. Notice in the close-up that the branches of the large background tree flow in a downward curve from the top point of the tree or tree trunk area. Each pine branch is slightly lower at its end than where it started at the tree trunk. If your board is in an upright position, the sky at the top, you will have to push this burned stroke away from you to create the proper curvature. Instead, turn your board upside down so the ground line is at the top of the board. Now you can easily pull the branch strokes toward you as you work.

Step 9: The pine trees are created with short dash strokes (Squares 1–5). These start at the edge of each tree branch and are pulled into the tree trunk.

Step 10: Turn the board upside down so that you are pulling the wood burning strokes toward you during this step. Begin the pine at the tip of the tree and work toward the ground. The dash strokes are clustered into small fan shapes to imply pine needle branches. Pull the strokes slowly to achieve a medium-dark coloring.

Step 11: Work the oak tree trunk and branches while you are holding the board upside down. Use a short scrubby-line stroke (Squares 61–64) to fill in the tree trunks. Again, work slowly to allow the burning to reach a medium-dark coloring.

Step 12: Outline the branches of the trees.

Step 13: As you work closer and closer to the canopy of the tree, the branches will become greater in number, shorter in length, and smaller in thickness than branches that lie close to the tree trunk. Be creative in how your finest branches twist, turn, and overlap each other.

This design is worked from the background to the foreground, beginning with the trees behind the church.

Form the branches and needles of the trees using dash strokes and scrubby lines.

Advanced Project Note

There are many times that a burning in a particular area is easier to accomplish by changing the working position of your board. Do not hesitate to change the position of your board so that your burned strokes are worked in a pulling movement, not a pushing motion. Pine trees and background tree branches are often easier to work upside down. By turning your board upside down to work the pine trees, your tool tip starts at the outer edge of the branch and then pulls toward you to the center of the tree. This makes the branch tips darker than the tree center and gives each branch a gentle curve.

Shade the small background pines and oak forest line.

Use a cooler temperature to burn the background pine trees to a lighter shade.

Advanced Project Note
You can lay cool-temperature, pale-value burning over the already worked dark-toned elements without disturbing those dark areas. This is a quick technique for background work because you can burn the trees that stand out within the background and then add your paler tones to fill in around them.

Step 14–18: Small background pines and oak forest line

Step 14: Behind the tall dark-toned pines and dark oaks is the far background grouping of pale-toned trees and pines. Reduce the setting on your tool to a cool temperature because you will want the burning in this area to be a pale value. Continue to work with your board upside down during this step.

Step 15: Work these far background pine trees exactly as you did the trees in Steps 7–13. Because the tool tip is at a cooler setting, these lines of the far background trees will naturally burn thinner than the first hot-temperature-burned pine trees.

Step 16: Random zigzags (Square 40) fill the space that represents the small oak trees in this background area.

Step 17: Once the area has been worked, add a second layer of random zigzags along the top edge of these trees to slightly darken them, defining the trees from the background pines.

Step 18: As you work these far background pines and small trees, you will come to sections that lie behind the dark pines and oaks burned in Steps 7–13. Because these tall pines and oaks were burned to a dark, heavy tonal value, you can allow your lighter burning texture in the far background work to touch and even cross over the darker work. The lighter-toned burning will not change or affect these darker burned areas.

Step 19–27: Church roofs and cross

Step 19: On a medium-high heat setting, outline along the front truss boards and side truss boards along the front edge of each roofline—the church's roof and the entry door's roof.

Step 20: Also outline the truss boards along the side roofs.

Step 21: Outline the cross. The top roofline and back side on both the church roof and the entry roof are not outlined at this stage. These two lines are worked later.

Step 22: With a short scrubby-line stroke, fill in the truss boards to a very dark shade of chocolate. They should be as dark as or darker than the background pines.

Step 23: The shingles on both roofs are first done by reducing your tool temperature to a cooler medium setting.

Step 24: Evenly spaced straight lines are pulled through the roof, parallel to the roof's bottom edge. These are broken lines; no one line goes the entire width of the roof. These long broken lines imply the rows of shingles.

Step 25: Add very short straight lines working parallel to the roof's side. These short lines imply the individual shingles and reach only from one row line to the next.

Step 26: Burn the top edge and back side edge of the roof during this step as if they were shingle lines. Use a broken line for these two areas.

Step 27: On the left side of the church roof and entry roof, you will see a small section of roof overhang. With a medium setting, fill this area with widely spaced straight lines that are parallel to the ground or bottom of your project board. This gives a light shadow to the underside of that overhang.

Outline the roof and cross, and then shade the shingles.

Use a short scrubby-line stroke to darken the truss boards to a black chocolate value.

Advanced Project Note
The church sits in the middle ground area of this design and is the main focus element of this project. This area, the middle ground, contains the darkest tonal values of the work. Notice in the finished sample that the shadow areas in the bushes beside the church and under the roof overhangs are the blackest tones. The background dark tones will be paler than the middle ground black tones.

Add shadow lines and guidelines with a 90-degree drafter's triangle, ruler, and a pencil.

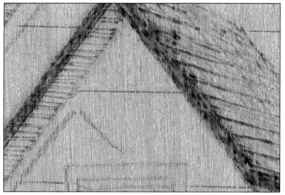

These guidelines will help in the placement of the shadows and wall planks.

Pull straight lines across the church walls to imply board planking.

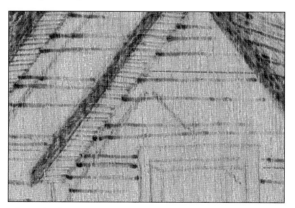

Allow the lines to be broken.

Step 28–30: Adding shadow lines and guidelines

Step 28: With a 90-degree drafter's triangle, ruler, and pencil, add a few guidelines to the pattern. Mark where the shadow from the roof would fall on the church's front wall.

Step 29: There is a wide shadow under the roof on the right side of the wall and a smaller, narrow shadow on the left side. Mark four guidelines on this front wall that are parallel to the board's bottom edge. These will help in the placement of the wall planks.

Step 30: A couple of wall plank guidelines are added to the church's side wall, parallel to the roof's bottom edge.

> **Advanced Project Note**
> As you are working on a project, you can create added guidelines or correct already traced pencil lines any time during the working process. Be flexible and creative in your art, making changes along the way as you develop the work.

Step 31–32: Detailing the siding boards

Step 31: Using a medium-high setting, begin pulling straight lines across the walls to imply the board planking. Just as with the roof shingle rows, allow these lines to be broken; not all of the planking lines need to go all the way from one side to the other.

Step 32: Where the board planking lines fall into the roof's shadow area, add a second layer of burning to darken the lines.

> **Advanced Project Note**
> You will notice in the close-up that I started these board plank lines at the wall edge and worked them toward the center of the wall. This places the darkest point of the line at the edge with the paler section toward the middle of the wall. Plan in advance where you want the burned line to begin. Use this tendency of the burn line's starting dark to your advantage.

Step 33–36: Roof overhang shadows

Step 33: The shadows on the front walls created by the roof overhang are laid in next. Allow the straight-line fill strokes to flow over the board planking lines. These lines are worked vertically to the bottom of the board.

Step 34: Reduce the heat setting to a low-medium temperature so that this new layer of shading will become lighter in tonal value than the overhead shadow and board planking you just burned in Steps 31 and 32.

Step 35: The shadows are created with vertical, tightly spaced straight lines.

Step 36: The narrow strip of shadow on the side wall underneath the roof line is also burned during this step.

Burn the shadow from the roof overhang with straight vertical lines.

> **Advanced Project Note**
> Just as with the background trees, this area was first worked with darker-toned detailing, then shadowed with a paler-toned burning. An added feature to this area is that the darker detail lines run in a different direction than the pale shading lines. By changing the direction of the shading line, you visually show that it is a different element—shadowing—not part of the wall planking. Had the shadow lines been worked in the same direction as the wall planking, the wall boards could have been overpowered by the numerous shade lines.

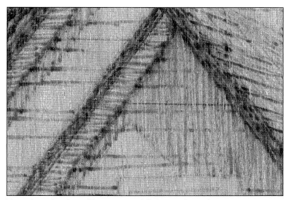
Use the shadow lines to guide your burning.

Step 37–38: Shading the front walls

Step 37: Because the sunlight is coming from the back of the church, the front wall of the church and the front wall of the entry are slightly darker than the side wall.

Step 38: Reduce the temperature of your tool to a cool setting, and using a short scrubby-line stroke, burn the entire area of both front walls to a pale tonal value. Because the board planking was burned to a dark tone and the shadows were created in a medium-dark tone, this pale tone can be worked right over top of the previous work without changing either area.

The front wall of the church is slightly darker than the side wall.

> **Advanced Project Note**
> By continually reducing the temperature of your tool tip, you can build up multiple layers of paler tones over medium and dark tones.

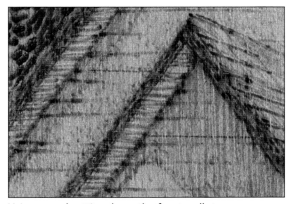
Using a cool setting, burn the front walls to a pale tonal value.

Detail the doors, windows, and walls on a medium cool setting.

Step 39–43: Detailing the doors, windows, and walls

Step 39: Turn your thermostat up slightly to a medium-cool setting.

Step 40: Fill in the door and the glass areas of the windows with a medium-toned scrubby-line stroke.

Step 41: Add outline detailing to the church along the sides where the corner trim boards lie. All of these outlines and those in the next step were worked in a medium to medium-hot setting.

Step 42: Outline the door and the windowsills.

Step 43: Shadow the left side of the door opening, inside the doorsill, with a medium-dark scrubby-line stroke.

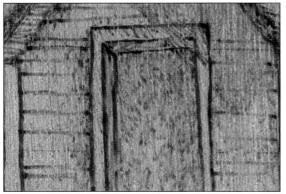

Use scrubby-line strokes to fill the door and the glass of the windows.

Advanced Project Note
Change your thermostat setting as needed so that you can control the tonal depth of each element within the area that you are burning. The side wall area of the church contains small areas of medium and medium-dark tones. Changing the temperature setting and working the area as a unit makes this area more coherent than burning some elements while your temperature is set on medium then returning to the wall later for the medium-dark elements.

Step 44–45: Adding door and entry shadows

Step 44: In the close-up photo, notice the very thin strip of shading on the church wall to the left of the entry. This shadow is created because the entry blocks that section of the wall from the sunlight. Burn a light layer of scrubby-line strokes along this thin strip to develop this shadow.

Step 45: Notice that this shadow runs along the church wall to the left of the entry roofline and the entry wall. A second shadow falls onto the entry's wall to the left of the door because of the doorjamb area. These two shadows are very small areas to work; however, it is this added shading detail that will give your work a more realistic impression when done.

Add subtle door and entry shadows to the burning.

Notice the small strips of shadow to the left of the entry wall and the doorjamb.

Advanced Project Note
Adding very fine details or extra-fine shading will dramatically add to the realism of your finished burning. Often, it is the small touches that turn a good woodburning into a great one.

Step 46–50: Stone foundation

Step 46: The stones in the foundation are made up of very tightly packed straight lines. As you work the stones, let each stone have its own direction for these lines.

Step 47: Use a higher temperature setting to make the front wall stones fairly dark.

Step 48: The stone foundation under the side wall is worked in the same manner but with a slightly reduced temperature.

Step 49: Along the top edge and left side of the foundation wall, add a light layering of scrubby-line shadows. These are done in a medium value.

Step 50: Go over the entire stone foundation with a second layering of scrubby-line strokes on medium-cool heat to tone the background of the stone foundation a pale value. You want the stones slightly darker than the surrounding foreground grass.

Advanced Project Note
You don't have to outline an area to create a realistic impression in that area. In the stone foundation, no individual stone is outlined. Instead, tightly packed straight lines are used to give the stones form and shape. Avoid giving your burnings a coloring book look with the overuse of outlines.

Burn the stone foundation of the church.

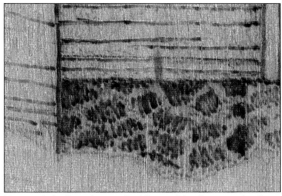
Use straight lines layered with scrubby lines to shade the stones.

Step 51–53: Large shrubs

Step 51: There are three large shrubs next to the church, with two on the left and one on the right. These are worked with a high temperature setting to create strong, dark lines. The texturing stroke is a long, gentle curve that starts at the tip of the shrub and moves toward the center. Create these lines in small clumps until you reach the ground.

Step 52: Once the entire shrub area has been filled, add a second layer of long, gentle curved-line clumps in the lower quarter of the shrub to dramatically blacken this section. This second layer will be more tightly packed to increase the black tones needed for the darkest shading of the scrubs next to the church walls.

Step 53: The ground shading in the far left scrub, at the ground line, is only worked to a medium-dark tone.

Advanced Project Note
The shading in the middle ground shrubs nearest the church is the blackest tone of the burning. You will notice that the two sections of this shrub shading, one on each side of the church, are directly adjacent to the very pale values of the church walls. This creates areas of sharp tonal contrast that attract the eye. The black of the shrub shadowing enhances the white-pale tones of the church, giving the church visual emphasis.

Use a high temperature to burn the large shrubs on both sides of the church.

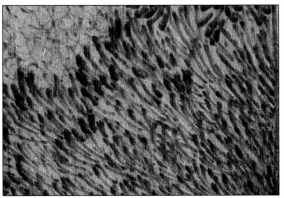
Layering and a high temperature create the dark values of these curved lines.

Shade the dirt around the stones in the path very heavily.

Step 54–55: Stepping stone path

Step 54: The burning on the stone path is worked in the areas surrounding the stepping stones. Only a few accent lines were added to the stones themselves.

Step 55: Use a random curl stroke for the dirt spaces. Set the tool tip to a medium-high temperature.

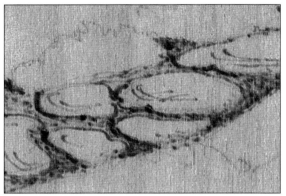

The stones themselves are not burned, except for a few accent lines.

Advanced Project Note

Because darker value tones have more visual impact than pale value tones, the stone walk area is worked very dark. This leads the eye along the stone path to the church door, which was worked in a much paler tone. Just as with the sharp contrast of dark and pale tones in the previous section that focus the eye on the church, you are now using dark tonal values to guide the eye to the most important point in the church: the entry door.

Step 56–57: Foreground grass

Step 56: Grass clumps are created with the same long curving lines that were used in the dark shrubs and are worked on a cool-medium setting. Turn the board upside down so that the grass lines are pulled from the ground line up to the tip of the grass blade. Let these lines form semi-circular fans for each clump.

Step 57: Not every area in the foreground needs burned grass clumps. For this sample, the grass clumps lie along the sides of the stone path, along the foundation of the church, and along the bottom of the background trees. Most of the foreground area has very little or no grass added.

Shade the foreground grass using long curving lines.

Advanced Project Note

Now you have firmly established the church as the focus of the burning, with the entry door as the most important element. Don't distract the eye with too many fine details or dark details in the foreground. Adding too many grass strokes or too many clumps of grass will pull the eye away from your focus point.

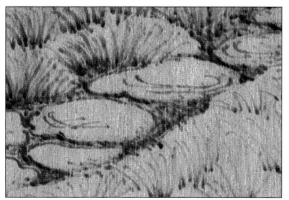

Use a semi-circular fan shape to create grass clumps.

Step 58–60: Large foreground grass clump

Step 58: To add just a little foreground focus, add a larger clump of grass to the lower right-hand corner of the design. The basic clump was burned exactly as the grass along the stone path and worked on the same cool-medium setting.

Step 59: Add a few seed heads by turning the board back into its upright position and adding a short, dark line stroke on top of each grass blade.

Step 60: A few wavy-line, wide grass blades finish the project.

A large clump of grass in the lower right corner adds foreground focus to the design.

Advanced Project Note

Add a little fun to your woodburning designs. The small foreground grass clumps with their seed heads give just a little surprise touch to the front area in the design. Because everything else in this scene is worked to give a general impression, the close-up detailing of each grass blade and the seed heads is unexpected.

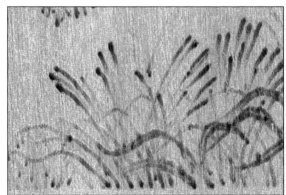

These wavy blades of grass were burned using long curved-line strokes.

Step 61–66: Finishing

Step 61: When the burning is complete, lightly sand the surface of the project with fine-grit sandpaper or a foam-core emery board to remove the roughness.

Step 62: Next, rub a white artist's eraser over the burning to remove any pencil lines from the original tracing.

Step 63: Dust your project well with either a lint-free cloth or a large drafter's dusting brush.

Step 64: Set your work where you can look over the project. Check that you have both very dark chocolate areas in the work as well as very pale linen colors to create contrast in the work. Are there middle tones of medium brown and coffee-with-cream shades? Does your church have a three-dimensional feeling? Even though you have worked through the steps of the project, new layering or shading can be added at this point to strengthen your design.

Step 65: This is an excellent time to sign and date your work in the lower right-hand corner.

Step 66: Once any touch-ups are finished, re-sand lightly, dust, and seal your project with either polyurethane or a paste wax.

The finished piece.

Cowboy Boots

© Lora S. Irish

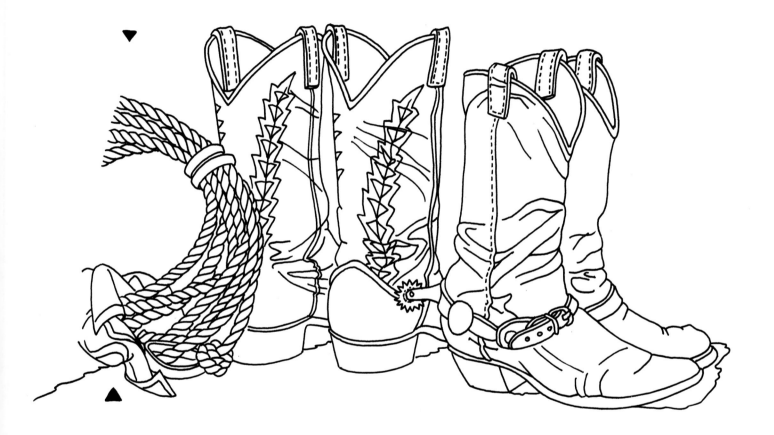

Cowboy Boots

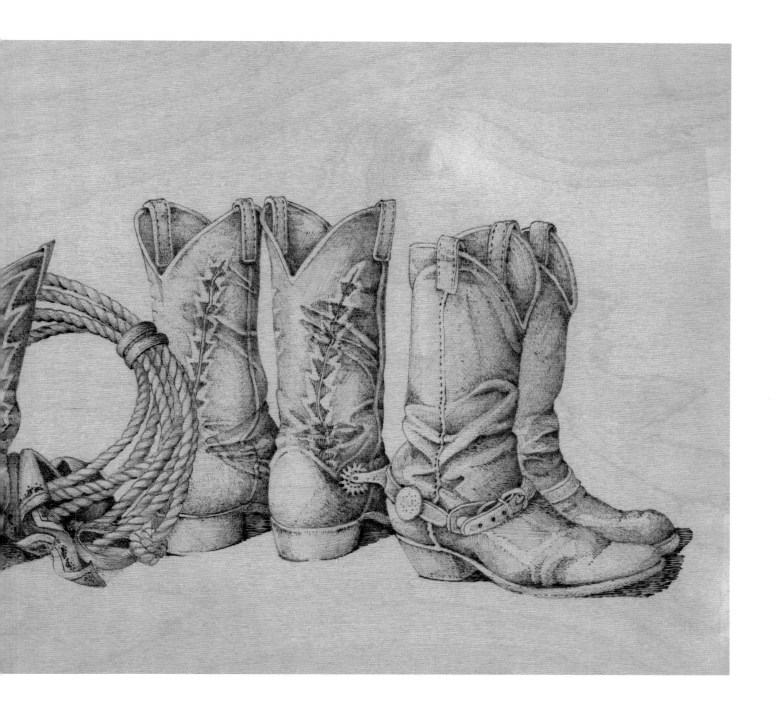

The Philadelphia Derringer

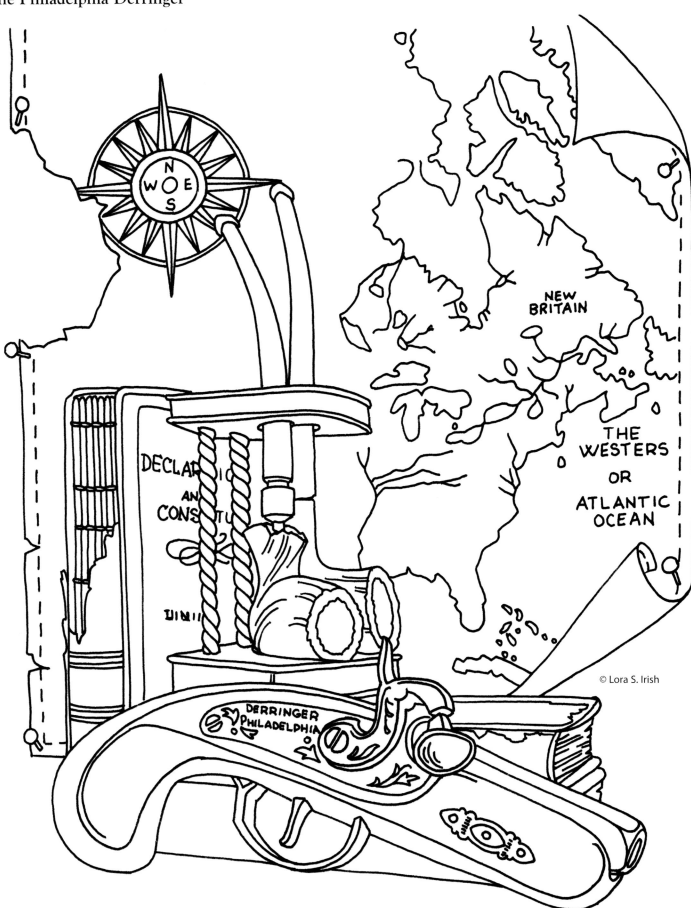

© Lora S. Irish

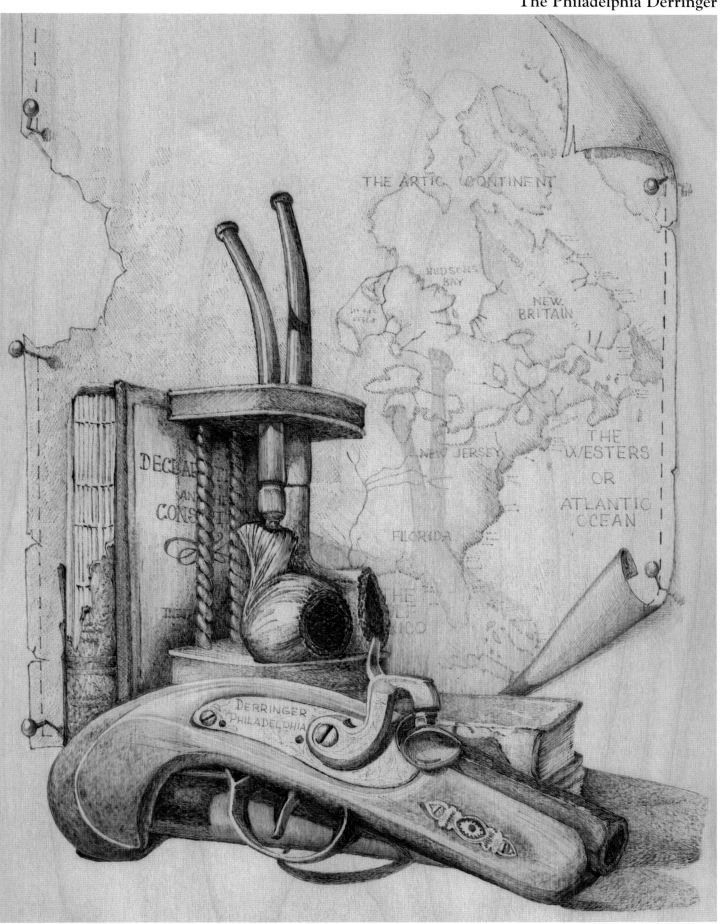

Western Dragon

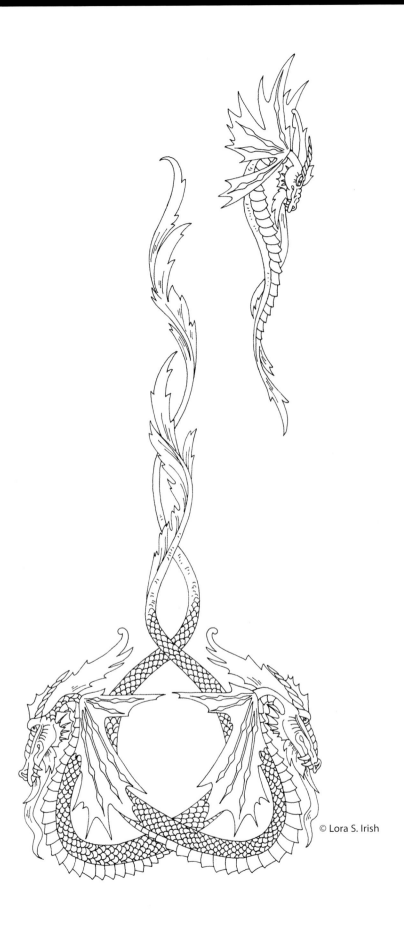

© Lora S. Irish

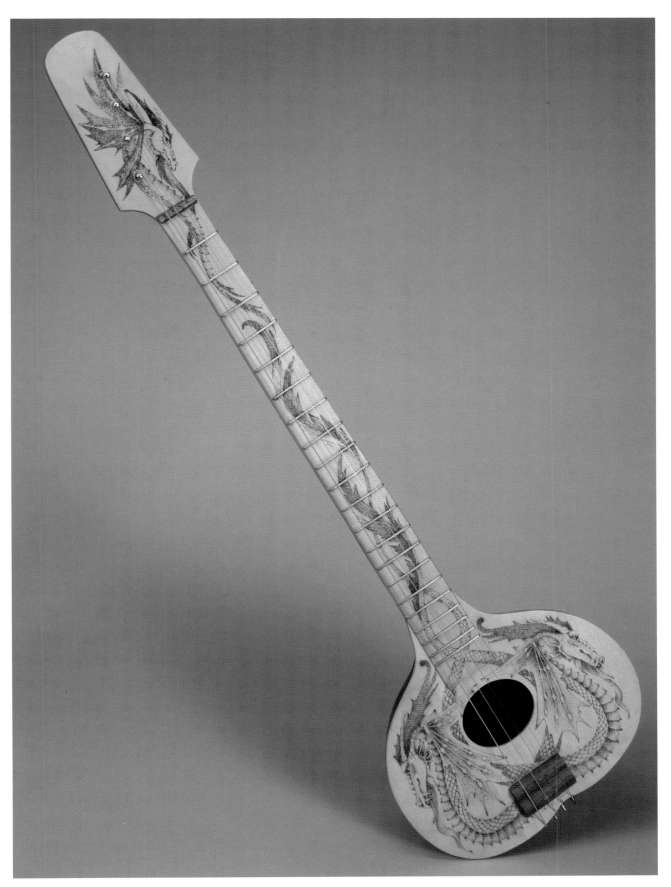

The End of the Road

© Lora S. Irish

Grandpa's Pride and Joy

© Lora S. Irish

Hide 'n Seek

© Lora S. Irish

Horned Owl

© Lora S. Irish

Harrisburg Star Barn

© Lora S. Irish

Our Town Mantel

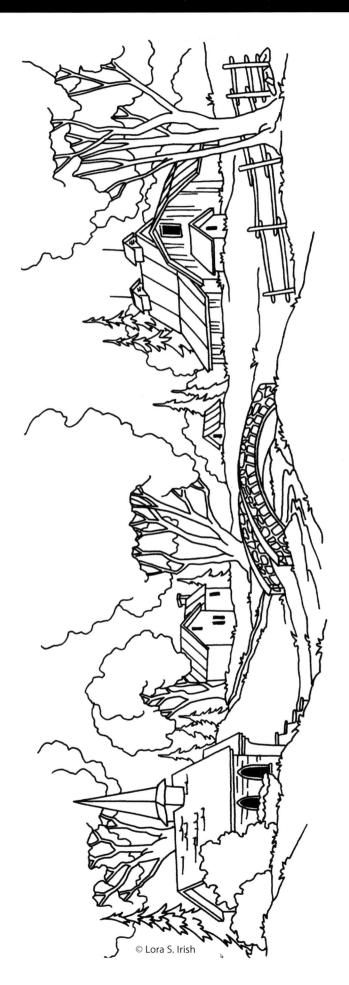

© Lora S. Irish

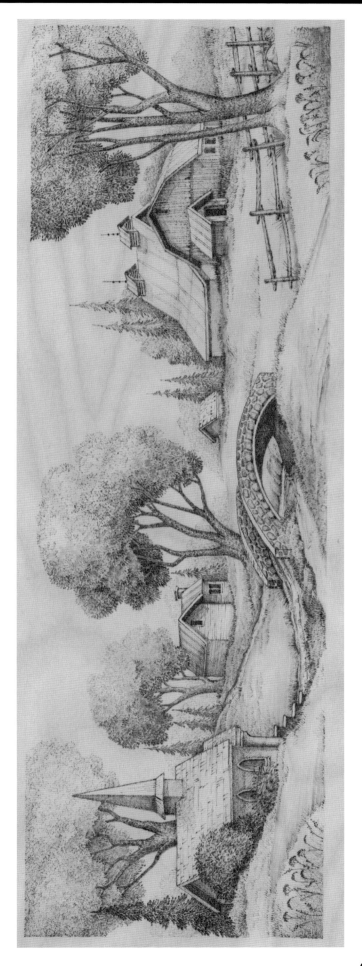

Our Town Mantel

Bank Barn

© Lora S. Irish

Church Mantel

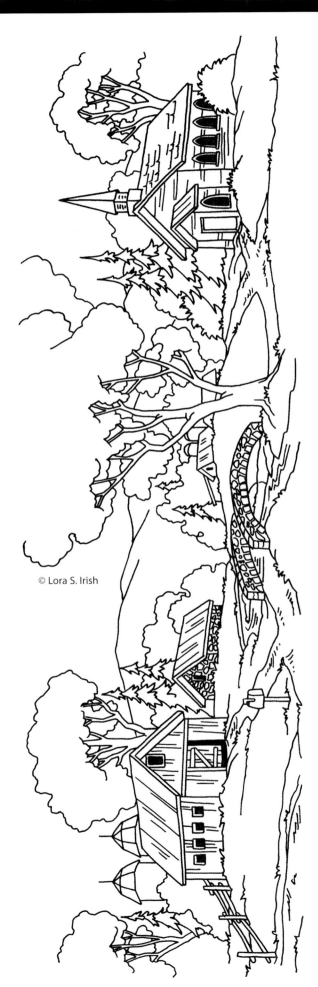

© Lora S. Irish

Glossary

Bleeding: Scorching of the wood surrounding the woodburner's tip beyond the area that you intend to burn. Bleeding is caused by burning at too hot a temperature. Also called haloing.

Calligraphy tip: A one-temperature tool tip used for writing letters.

Cone tip: A one-temperature tool tip used for creating fine detailing.

Contrast: The difference between two tonal values. The strongest contrast is created when white values directly touch the blackest values.

Element: An individual piece or part of a pattern or design. For example, grass, trees, and barn complexes are all elements in a landscape burning. Also called positive element.

End-grain: A piece of wood cut across the tree rings instead of with the grain. This cut of wood is harder to color than plain grain and has many imperfections that will show through the woodburning.

Flat shader: A variable-temperature tool tip used for shading.

Flow tip: A one-temperature tool tip used for large area fills.

Gradient tones: A tonal value area that blends from a pale tone into a dark tone or from a dark tone into a pale tone. This area shows all of the tones in between the starting tone and the ending tone.

Heartwood: The center part of a tree that has tighter grain lines and a darker coloring than sapwood.

Layers or layering: The process of reworking an area with multiple burnings of the same texture. Each layer is not burned directly on top of the others, but rotated slightly in order to burn a different area. These multiple burnings allow the artist a controlled means to gradually darken the area.

Large shading tip: A one-temperature tool tip used for shading large areas and shadows.

Large wire loop tip: A variable-temperature tool tip used for basic writing functions.

Lightfast: Resists fading from light.

Monochromatic: One color. Also includes the use of different tonal values of that color. Woodburnings are monochromatic works of the color brown using shades from pale beige through black chocolate.

Negative space: The area surrounding an element in a pattern. For example, the air around a mountain is negative space.

One-temperature tool: A woodburning tool that heats to only one temperature—high. These tools use a cast solid brass tip that has screw threads for mounting to the tool body. One-temperature tools are good for beginners and are easily found at most craft stores for an inexpensive price.

Plain grain: A piece of wood cut with the grain of the tree, not across the rings. This cut of wood is relatively easy to color with paints or coloring pencils.

Sapwood: This part of the tree surrounds the heartwood. It is lighter and has wider grain bands than the heartwood.

Sepia: Shades of brown ranging from very pale beige through black-brown tones.

Sepia scale: A chart marking each gradient of tonal value from the palest white value through the darkest black value, using brown tones.

Small round tip: A variable-temperature tool tip used for shading and fine detail.

Textures: Small repeating patterns of burned lines that add interest throughout the work, such as curly lines, circles, wavy lines, and short dashes. The term "texture" throughout this book refers to visual patterns, not actual physical texture created by high temperature burns.

Tonal values: The shades of a color created by adjusting the amount of white or black that a color contains. For woodburning, the tonal values range from very pale beige through black-brown shades. Pale tonal values like cream or beige contain large amounts of white mixed with brown. Dark tones, like dark chocolate, contain large amounts of black mixed with brown.

Universal tip: A one-temperature tool tip used for fine-line work as well as shading

Variable-temperature tool: A woodburning system that incorporates a variable-setting thermostat with the woodburning pen. This allows control over the color value of a burned area by changing the thermostat setting. Variable-temperature tools use a bent wire tip that can be either permanently fixed to the pen or interchangeable. This type of tool is a more advanced alternative to the one-temperature tool; however, it is also more expensive.

Vellum: Tracing paper.

Writing tip: A variable-temperature tool tip used for writing.

Index

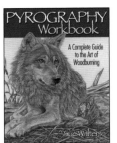
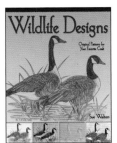
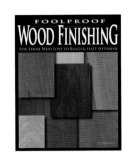

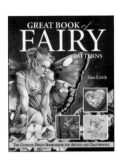

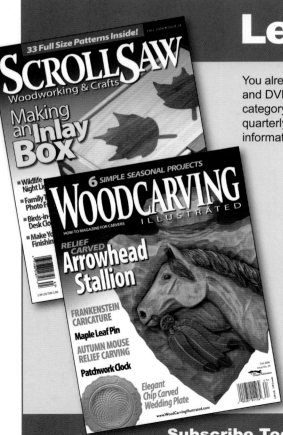